D1697070

Proceedings of the 2nd International Conference of Drug Regulatory Authorities

Organized by the Italian Ministry of Health

**Sponsored by the
World Health Organization**

**April 27 - 30, 1982
Rome, Italy**

Edited by

Duilio Poggiolini
General Director Pharmaceutical Division
Ministry of Health, Rome

Published by

Italian Ministry of Health

Rome, Italy

Distributed by

Raven Press

New York, N.Y.

Published by

MINISTRY OF HEALTH
VIALE DELLA CIVILTÀ ROMANA, 7 - ROME, ITALY

Distributed by

RAVEN PRESS
1140 AVENUE OF THE AMERICAS
NEW YORK, NEW YORK 10036

Copyright 1983 by Ministry of Health (Rome, Italy)

All rights reserved

NO PART OF THIS BOOK MAY BE REPRODUCED IN ANY FORM BY
PHOTOSTAT, MICROFILM, OR BY ANY OTHER MEANS, WITHOUT
WRITTEN PERMISSION FROM THE PUBLISHERS

International Standard Book Number 0-89004-995-5
Library of Congress Catalog Number 83-60594

Printed in Italy by Christengraf
Via Anagnina, 432a - Rome, Italy

CONTENTS

Contents

Contents

V

WELCOMING REMARKS

R. Altissimo

Minister of Health, Italy

It is indeed a great pleasure for me to open this Second International Conference of Drug Regulatory Authorities.

By organising this Conference, the Ministry of Health hopes to give a tangible and fruitful contribution to the policy of international co-operation which it has always tried to up-hold. I also take personal satisfaction from the realisation that this series of conferences actually originates from an initiative by our own Ministry, dating back to 1979 when the conference on Drug Regulation Harmonisation at Community level was organised right here in Rome. Even at that first Conference, the presence of extra-Communitary guests created a decidedly international atmosphere. This gave origin to the 1st International Conference held in Annapolis, Maryland in 1980, which proved to be such a success that this 2nd Conference in Rome was proposed.

I must, at this point, offer a particular vote of thanks to WHO for its sponsorship. The Italian government is greatly honoured by this, and also encouraged in its efforts to attain advanced forms of international cooperation, especially regarding developing countries. WHO's sponsorship will, without doubt, contribute greatly to the success of this meeting.

It is certainly a unique and exceptional occasion to find gathered together here such a large number of Drug Regulatory Authorities from all over the world, and I must take this opportunity to highlight some of the features which give this Conference special significance. We are all aware of the paramount importance of drug regulation, and its great relevance due to the impact it has on public opinion. Above all, it must be ascertained that drugs are effective, have given requirements of quality, and may be used safely. On the other hand, by its very definition, a medicinal product is a matter which concerns everybody's health, and as such, it cannot be limited to national interests and becomes a decidedly international problem. The fact is, a drug's impact does not concern only the country of origin or where it is produced, but extends to all nations who may be interested in its use. With this in mind, recent years have witnessed the development of an always more extensive communication between various authorities and administrations responsible for drug regulation. I am proud to say that Italy was among the countries who felt this problem deeply, and has been active in promoting such cooperation.

Only as little as five years ago, there still existed a barrier between one country and another, and a reluctance to encourage inter-country communication and consultation, to the extent that some very serious decisions on drugs could be reached in one country without others even knowing about them. This obviously gave rise to unfavourable consequences, and the public did not feel adequately protected when such decisions became known. The public could rightfully wonder why the administration in one country should take certain measures, while its own administration appeared to remain insensitive and inactive.

However, this was not the only element that contributed toward greater collaboration among drug regulatory authorities.

There is the need to have drugs available, quickly and in sufficient quantities to serve everybody's requirements. Society looks for therapeutical means for defeating diseases not yet eliminated, and especially those that are even on the increase. Hence the incentive to reach harmonisation of criteria and regulations, the need to avoid obstacles and misunderstandings, and to make available to all nations any safe and effective drug already available to one nation.

When I previously mentioned " five years ago ", I did not use that time period at random. My choice was motivated by the fact that, just five years ago, the European Economic Community put into effect its great experiment to reach harmonisation of pharmaceutical laws and regulations among the member countries. This trend, started within the E.E.C., led to the establishment of the Brussels Committee for Proprietary Medicinal Products, which provides on pharmaceutical regulation policy and therefore, supervises the so-called " European Registration "; that is, the authorisation granted by one communitary country to market a given product should be valid for all the E.E.C. member states.

The European initiative was the stimulus for a consultation movement at world-wide level with two basic aims: — complete and speedy knowledge of measures taken regarding drugs in other countries, and to attain greater similarity in regulations, authorisations and registrations of drugs to be marketed. To these two basic aims, we may add another. Developing countries today are eager for information, advice, and the possibility of availing themselves of the technical effort already made by other countries. Obviously, they demand that the drugs imported into their countries offer all the due guarantees of safety and efficacy. Therefore, exporting countries should supply all the technical elements required for such assessments.

For this reason, this Conference has brought together delegations from developed and developing countries; representatives from countries all over the world are gathered around the same table. The results of efforts in consultation and harmonisation recently made, in particular during the Cancun Conference, have great meaning, apart from their success, in the fact of their having been founded on the confrontation of experiences of both developed and developing countries.

It is my opinion that such exigencies are most deeply felt in the pharmaceutical and medical fields. The elements leading to making a drug available to the public are indeed complex, and the trend should be to ensure the availability of valid therapeutical means to all the countries of the world. Finally, I wish to emphasise that harmonisation of drug regulation is absolutely necessary to facilitate research and to simplify procedures. This is of vital interest today because the request for innovation is world-wide, and the starting point of innovation is research.

In other words, the development of tomorrow's medicine depends on putting into effect sound and wise regulations today, in order to avoid, above all, useless waste and repetition of research. Therefore, if we wish to obtain effective and safe drugs for the future, we must all collaborate now.

Now, I am sure, you are eager to get our discussions underway, and I can only offer my warmest wishes of welcome to all of you, some of you from very distant countries, and all linked by the common will to cooperate and attain positive results, taking into account different needs, towards a higher level of public health.

INTRODUCTION TO THE SECOND I.C.D.R.A.

D. Poggiolini

General Director Pharmaceutical Division, Ministry of Health, Italy

To introduce the Second International Conference of Drug Regulatory Authorities is for me a gratifying task. The preparation of this meeting involved quite a lot of organization efforts which proved necessary to ensure the Conference and all its participants a certain degree of functionality and comfort which, I hope, will meet everybody's satisfaction. But to see gathered here in Rome the drug regulatory authorities of all parts of the world is, for the Italian Ministry of Health and for me personally, a really gratifying event and a source of great satisfaction.

I would like, first of all, to thank once more all those who, throughout the whole world, have actively cooperated toward the success of the meeting, and in particular I wish to express my warmest thanks to W.H.O., the high sponsorship of which is determining for the success of the Conference. I thank also all those who have generously provided sound advice and suggestions.

We had in fact the intention of organizing this Conference by asking for the advice and observations of all its participants. This implied that the contacts had to be entered into starting from the list of the countries which participated in the Annapolis Conference. Subsequently, during the consultation phase, other countries were added and finally the official invitations were sent out to all W.H.O. member states.

Now, 44 countries, and 5 international organizations are present here and I am pleased to thank them all very much.

In a very special way I wish to thank the Advisory Board for its valuable contribution given us by letter and through the meeting held in Brussels on December 8, 1981, which set in motion the final phases of the Conference organization.

We are obviously all well aware that the persons who gave this contribution are worthy of high praise as regards international pharmaceutical cooperation toward which, they have been actively working for a long time. And I am pleased to say that in these recent years international cooperation in the pharmaceutical field has known an always more intense and wide expansion.

In my opinion, pharmaceutical cooperation is an evolutive process which begins in the present situation and will give its fruits in the future. The only thing we cannot determine is if this future will be near or far.

In this connection, I only wish to set forth, on the basis of my personal experience, some steps which I believe to be very important in the evolution of harmonization.

First of all, we have to find reasonable motives for harmonization. I think that the best approach to this matter is the examination of some data drawn from the study of the international pharmaceutical market.

These data should discriminate two types of pharmaceutical products.

a) *Those having a limited circulation*: they are products of minor importance from the therapeutic point of view and do not represent a remarkably advanced step towards pharmacology progress. Their circulation is therefore limited to one or two countries, according to local environment and conditions.

b) *The ones having a worldwide circulation*: they are mostly remarkable innovations, which can steadily be found in several countries, and they form therefore a real international market.

We have to state that the greatest part of new products, which are the outcome of research in a limited number of countries will, sooner or later, be found on the markets of all the other countries. In fact pharmaceutical innovation tends to spread very quickly in all countries and in particular in the more developed ones, and this just because in the latter the request for innovation is more active.

In any case, the goal to be reached by drug regulatory authorities is to ensure the quality, safety and efficacy of these drugs under similar standards.

These goals should, therefore, be reached for products spread all over the world, avoiding the repetition of test and approval procedures, which delays their availability and hinders the development of therapeutic innovation.

The importance of innovation in pharmaceutical research is a point on which obviously you all will agree. It is in fact the sustaining pillar of any future development of therapy. It has therefore to be fostered and promoted in any possible way according to the requirement of a higher degree of safety.

It follows that our efforts should aim at cutting down all obstacles still hindering the development of this activity all over the world.

On the other hand, the pharmaceutical regulatory procedures followed up to now in the various countries are generally based on the approach of autonomy of judgement and decision.

This attitude in fact, based on the justified need to provide suitable safety protection to the respective populations' health, actually results in a series of very often repeated assessments on the same matter, generally accompanied by the request for tests which have already been carried out in the country of origin.

At this point it might be useful to consider whether the motive driving the different countries to repeat the various checks and controls, and sometimes asking the manufacturer to carry out new tests in the country where the marketing of the new product is requested, are really founded on scientific reasons or if they are due to political motivations, among which to be kept under consideration are those regarding the reciprocity of treatment.

And finally, we cannot forget the problem of the less developed countries which are not always able to ensure their own evaluation of drugs and depend on the information given by developed and exporting countries.

In conclusion, I believe that there are reasonable grounds for harmonization of the sector. How can we reach this goal? I think that the problem of harmonization should be considered by dividing it into progressive steps, which I submit to your reflection.

In my opinion, anyhow, we have to bear in mind that each step is the basis for the following one, in a very precise order. In other words, it is impossible to reach a full harmonization without completely going along this progressive way.

The progressive steps of harmonization could pass through the following phases:

a) common rules and criteria for chemical, pharmacological, toxicological and clinical tests;

b) common interpretation of technical data;

c) familiarization among drug regulatory authorities;

d) close consultation among drug regulatory authorities before decision making;

e) agreement among the various countries for a mutual recognition of the drug authorization.

Keeping in mind these approaches, particularly helpful to their realization were last years' international conferences which, I may say, represent the various stages towards the achievement of our common goal.

I must say that for me it is a motive of satisfaction to remember that the meeting of a group of drug regulatory authorities was for the first time promoted and organized on the initiative of the Italian Ministry of Health. I am referring to the Symposium on the " Future of procedures for the harmonization of drug registration in the E.E.C. ", held in Rome during June 1979.

Object of that Meeting was mainly the question of the free drug circulation in the European Common Market. However, the presence among the invited authorities of greatly welcome guests belonging to non-communitary countries (United States, Switzerland, Sweden) immediately indicated how it was absolutely necessary that every question pertaining to drug regulation and harmonization be internationally and world-wide extended.

That Rome Meeting followed a different trend inasmuch as — being open to the public — it made possible a frank confrontation of the thesis set forth by the various speakers.

I dare say that the best proof of our initiative's success was undoubtedly the stimulus it created to realize the International Conference of Drug Regulation Authorities which was organized by F.D.A. and W.H.O. and held in Annapolis (United States) during October 1980.

For the first time, in October 1980 representatives of some 25 Nations from all parts of the world were all gathered together, in spite of differences in language, culture, economic and industrial activity, governmental structure, and health needs, showing a common desire to secure for their peoples the safest and most effective array of medicines that science can provide.

The Annapolis Meeting improved communication and cooperation among the community of people charged with the regulation of the world's drug supply and thus it improved effectiveness and efficiency of drug regulation in each of our countries.

The Annapolis Meeting also showed that communication among us is of paramount importance.

But, as Dr. Goyan said, communication is a means, not an end. And that emphasises the very considerable success reached by the second portion of the Annapolis Conference dealing with the harmonization of regulatory requirements.

The crucial point of the Annapolis Meeting was, however, to realize that the information each nation requires in the service of effective drug regulation can be vastly more useful if it is widely spread, especially throughout less developed countries.

At Annapolis it immediately became clear that such a conference was to be the first of a series of meetings of the same kind. Then and therefore the Italian delegation had the honour to ask that the second conference be held in Rome. Why this request? First of all to immediately strengthen the spirit of a tradition on the basis of which the present meeting (which we shall define the Second I.C.D.R.A.) is actually the third of a series which we hope will be long and rich in satisfactory results; secondly, because we think that the universal character of the Eternal City offers the most favourable atmosphere to the gathering of so many countries' representatives and to their civil and cultural exchanges; and finally because we Italians believe we deserve a first ranking place with regard to the efforts aiming at pharmaceutical harmonization. I think you all know how much I personally, and on many occasions, exerted myself to make it understood that, notwithstanding social and economic differences existing among the various countries, no pharmaceutical problem is really restricted to only one country.

It is therefore a great satisfaction for us to have the Second I.C.D.R.A. held in Rome.

The Conference has been set up according to the following lines:

1) organization by the Italian Ministry of Health and sponsorship of W.H.O.;

2) invitations sent out to all W.H.O. member states:

3) participation of delegates appointed by the respective governmental authorities.

The basic theme of this Conference is the survey of international aspects of national drug regulation.

Multifarious are the aspects to be examined during the course of work.

A large number of W.H.O. member states currently have no possibility of establishing and maintaining fully-staffed drug regulatory agencies. They are therefore dependent to a large extent on decisions, as to the quality, efficacy and safety of drugs, taken by regulatory agencies in large developed countries. It is therefore important to determine to what extent national decisions can be regarded as scientifically valid for other parts of the world, how such decisions and the motives underlying them can be internationally disseminated, and what measures drug exporting countries take to ensure quality, safety and efficacy of the drugs they export. It is also necessary to examine models for effective regulatory operation in countries having limited resources.

In addition to dealing with this main theme, the meeting will provide an opportunity for agencies to exchange information and news on current scientific problems.

Participants have been asked to submit in advance to the Conference Secretary a list of the subjects to be discussed so that the preliminary Agenda could be prepared.

I have to thank all the countries which sent us the list of items to be discussed. This has enabled us to prepare an Agenda of work divided into three sections:

1) safety items; 2) efficacy items; 3) policy items.

The Conference is organized in sessions, panels and groups of work.

As you know, the Conference is closed to the press, industry observers and the public, in order to facilitate a frank exchange of ideas. An open meeting has been organized, at 3 p.m., at the end of the Conference, for a discussion on the Conference outcome, during which the conclusions of the Meeting will be submitted to interested parties for information and discussion. We have, in fact, considered it useful that the interested parties be acquainted with the proceedings of this Conference.

I, in fact, strongly believe that an exchange of ideas and proposals with the interested parties who have agreed to attend the last day open meeting could bear valuable fruit and give rise to future activities, decided and achieved together with the pharmaceutical industry, in the higher interest of public health.

I think that now I can only conclude my intervention by stating my firm-belief that the Second I.C.D.R.A. will be a further step in the long process for the creation of a real atmosphere of cooperation and fruitful coordination among all the drug regulatory authorities and, above all, a mutual confrontation and exchange among developed and developing countries.

It is without doubt that, as years go by, we will see that a real community of drug regulatory authorities is being formed. These authorities have

D. Poggiolini

a rôle of paramount importance for their responsibilities, which are scientific and technical, as well as political. However the main goal of their activity must be to guarantee the health of the people in the countries where they perform their functions.

Now this responsibility is becoming more and more an international fact.

With this awareness and this concern the drug regulatory authorities attending this meeting, and all the others who, though agreeing with these principles, are unable to be physically present, are setting about to carry out their work during this Conference.

My sincere wish is that these Roman days will prove to be fruitful in making a step forward in our hard task and worthy of being repeated.

MESSAGE FROM WHO

J. Dunne

WHO, Geneva

The generosity of the Ministry of Health of Italy in sponsoring and organizing this Second International Conference of Drug Regulatory Authorities has provided a vital stimulus to the efforts of the World Health Organization and the collectivity of its Member States to advance standards of drug control. Accordingly, I need hardly stress, on behalf of the Director-General of WHO, Dr Halfdan Mahler, that the Organization's interest in co-sponsoring this congress extends far beyond mere symbolism. Recommendations formulated during this meeting will have immediate relevance for WHO in its efforts to adapt its programmes and activities to the best advantage of regulatory authorities in both developed and developing countries.

The first conference of this series, which was organized by the Food and Drug Administration of the United States of America in Annapolis, Maryland in October 1980, offered an unprecedented occasion for officials responsible for drug control in countries at all stages of development to discuss means of constructive collaboration. The meeting left no doubt that, in order to perform their statutory functions with confidence, the large majority of countries were to a considerable degree dependent upon knowledge of decisions taken elsewhere, and that even highly evolved agencies gained benefit from efficient interchange of information. It was manifestly apparent, however, that the domestically-oriented terms of reference provided to national regulatory authorities, and the confidentiality widely applied to privileged information they receive from private sources can, on occasion frustrate intercommunication. Moreover, it was also generally acknowledged that the extent to which available channels of communication have been exploited, and notably the WHO Certification Scheme for Drugs moving in International Commerce, fall disappointingly short of earlier aspirations.

The participants at this conference today are obviously expectant that direct discussion of mutual problems will foster improvement in communication. The groundwork was laid at Annapolis but it is crucially important to maintain the momentum and to establish these conferences as biennial gatherings. Professor Duilio Poggiolini's pledge, given in Annapolis on behalf of the Italian Government, to convene the current meeting here in Rome has tangibly advanced the realisation of that aspiration. We are profoundly appreciative of his efforts in planning this meeting, and we are as gratified as he must be that they have been rewarded by the attendance here of representatives of 44 countries drawn from each of the six WHO regions. This, of itself, is evidence that an international perspective in drug control is not only discernible but that it is established as a necessary element in its infrastructure.

DRUG ASSESSMENT IN EUROPE

NOTE ON REGULATORY CONTROL IN FRANCE

J. Dangoumau * and M. Legrain **

Directeur de la Pharmacie et du Médicament
President de la Commission d'Autorisation de Mise sur le Marché, AMM

Legislative Basis of The Control

The requirements to secure that all medicines, whether manufactured in France or imported, are of good quality and in accordance with the requirements and specifications set up by France and the EEC, are included in various legislative and administrative decisions.

French pharmaceutical Law is based on the Act of 1941 and Ordonnance of 1959. Requirements are included in the " Code of Public Health ". More recently to reinforce security and quality specifications and to adhere to EEC regulations, many legislative and administrative decisions have been made, for example:

— The " Ordonnance of September 1967 on Drug Marketing Licence with application Orders of

- November 21, 1972,

- February 9, 1978

- September 20, 1978

— The Act of July 7, 1980, with application Order of October 3, 1980 on post marketing surveillance.

— The Act of January 3, 1972, with application Order of August 26, 1976 to control information and advertising on Drugs.

The pharmaceutical Acts cover the field of all medicines including biological products, plants for pharmaceutical use and homeopathic drugs.

Administrative Structure

The Pharmacy and Drugs Directorate (Direction de la Pharmacie et du Médicament) employs 145 persons including pharmacists, physicians and administrative staff.

The Minister of Health and the Pharmacy and Drugs Directorate are helped by Consultants working on a voluntary non-remunerated basis in various *sciéntific specialist Committees*. The number of persons working as Members of Committees or as Experts advising the Committees is around 250. The mission of such an advanced scientific apparatus is to give the national community and countries importing French drugs all the guarantees it is entitled to demand in agreement with the latest technical and scientific requirements.

In agreement with the French Law all decisions are made by the Minister of Health. In fact the scientific advice of various Committees have always been followed by the Administration.

A special Department of the Pharmacy Directorate is the '' Inspection de la Pharmacie ''. The Inspectors are in charge of the control of pharmaceutical enterprises. Annual inspection of all manufacturers are routinely performed and more frequent inspections are possible on request from the Pharmacy Directorate. Inspectors have to check that the Good Manufacturing Practice (GMP of the WHO and the EEC regulation) are adequately followed. Special courses for the Inspectors on GMP, toxicological studies... are regularly planned.

Inspectors are in charge both of the control of distribution including warehousing and retail outlets as well as of the surveillance of routes of supply. In France, all drugs are sold only in pharmacies whether under medical prescription or not. Free sale of drugs is forbidden.

Process of Licensing New Drug. The '' AMM '' Committee

Aims of the Committee

The Drug Licensing Committee was set up to advise the Ministry of Health. In a statement issued to the press on 21 February 1978, at the time of the Committee's creation, the Ministry of Health gave the following explanation:

'' The setting up of this new Committee will make it possible to pursue an active policy in licensing both old and new pharmaceutical products. The Committee will be responsible in particular for ensuring that products are of therapeutic value and also that they are properly used since the licenses include a precise description of the therapeutic indications, dosage, contra-indications and precautions. It will therefore have a direct influence on the number of products and be able to guide their use.

The Committee's unquestionable authority and independence will enable it to give its advice in full agreement with the medical profession and pharmaceutical industry after a full hearing, similar to the procedure adopted in a number of other countries, involving consultation with experts and with the laboratories responsible for bringing the drugs onto the market ".

The Committee is a sort of " last filter ", guaranteeing the safety and efficacy of a drug before it is brought onto the market. The standards applied are determined by present scientific knowledge as it appears from the work of international bodies.

The working of the Committee

The Committee includes twelve regular members and twelve deputy members nominated in relation with their scientific competence by the Minister of Health plus the Director of Pharmacy, the Director of the National Research Institute (INSERM) and the Director of the National Health Laboratory. The following method of work has been adopted: two groups work on a complementary basis — the Full Committee and the Permanent Working Group.

The Committee meets in plenary session once every fortnight. The aim of these meetings is:

— to study in detail all important dossiers concerning new licence applications, licences for drugs with an identical active principle (generic products), changes of formula, etc... and to take decisions after hearing evidence from specialist rapporteurs.

— to define an agreed policy making it possible to deal fairly with all pending and future cases.

— to give a hearing to representatives of pharmaceutical laboratories under the appeal procedure.

The Permanent Working Group meets once every fortnight, alternating with the Full Committee. Its dual role is to dispatch the minor cases and to sort out the more difficult ones before they are studied in plenary session.

All the working group's findings are submitted to the Full Committee for approval.

The rapporteurs

They are chosen by the Pharmacy and Drugs Directorate on the Committee's recommendation. Their role is to carry out an in-depth study of the analytical, toxicological, pharmacological and clinical dossier compiled by the laboratory and to report on their findings to the Committee. Depending on the importance of the dossier, assessed from the point of view of originality, efficacy and safety, the number of rapporteurs appointed varies from one to five. The rapporteurs are called upon to assist the Committee in its appeal decisions.

Scientific and technical reports

Part of the Committee's information is based on the hearing and discussion of synthetic reports drawn up by its members and, if necessary, by non-members.

The working groups

Their objective is to study problems on which the Committee requires additional information in order to define a policy. The working groups are composed of representatives of the Pharmacy and Drugs Directorate, Members of the Committee and Experts chosen for their qualification in the field under consideration. Three working groups on analgesics, antibiotics and non-steroidal anti-inflammatory drugs met regularly during the past years. Two working groups, one on " plants " used as medicine and one on " genetic engineering " and drug manufacturing have recently been organized.

The dossiers and clinical trials

All dossiers are studied according to a " one step " procedure. Decisions of the AMM Committee are taken within a four months period after deposit of the completed dossier by the Pharmaceutical Firm at the Ministry of Health.

All dossiers for a new drug application are divided in four parts: Analytical data, toxicological, pharmacological and clinical data.

Clinical trials are performed under the responsability of the Firm and her Experts. The Minister of Health is informed of the decision to perform clinical trials on new drugs. Advice of ethical Committees is strongly encouraged. In 1981, 560 requests to perform clinical trials were registered. The very delicate problem raised by experiments on healthy volunteers will be re-examined in a near future by the bodies concerned.

Relationship between the AMM Committee
and other bodies concerned by drugs

The AMM Committee, located at the base of this scientific and administrative apparatus, was given the task of establishing a close collaboration with all Committees concerned with drugs. This collaboration is furthered by the fact that the Scientific and Technical Secretariat of each of these Committees is provided by the Pharmacy and Drugs Directorate. The fact that AMM Committee members sit on other Committees is also an excellent guarantee of good mutual information at the service of a joint policy.

Relation with the National Pharmacopoeia Committee. The rules of quality relating, in particular, to excipients, active principles and recipients are laid down in the Pharmacopoeia. Conversely, the AMM Committee can ask the Pharmacopoeia to define more accurately or strengthen existing standards.

Relation with the Technical Drug Monitoring Board (Commission de la Pharmacovigilance). Ministerial decisions taken on the Drug Monitoring

Board's advice have a direct impact on AMM decisions, which may have to be revised. We shall mention, by way of example, the problems caused to the two Committees by bismuth, clioquinol, tienilic acid, etc...

Relation with the Transparence Committee. This Committee has the responsibility to define from data of the licensing dossier advantages and drawbacks of any new drug as far as security and efficacy are concerned, taking into consideration therapeutic drugs already available on the market. The Committee controls the Transparence sheet now routinely distributed to all French physicians.

Relations with the Committee responsible for controlling and revising the dictionaries of pharmaceutical preparations (Dictionnaire VIDAL). This Committee's work will be facilitated in so far as a very precise drafting of indications and contra-indications, taking into account the most up-to-date scientific data, will be provided in the framework of the AMM license. This comment also applies to the *Advertising Control Committee.*

Relations with Institutes and Laboratories concerned with drugs. Two bodies, INSERM (Institut National de la Santé et de la Recherche Médicale - National Institute of Health and Medical Research) and the Laboratoire National de Santé (National Health Laboratory) are represented on the Committee under its statutes. INSERM's technical and scientific expertise is widely utilized to elucidate the various problems relating to the toxicological, pharmacological and clinical evolution of pharmaceutical preparations. INSERM supplies the Committee with expert information and, if necessary, assumes the role of rapporteur through its experts.

The collaboration between the National Health Laboratory and the Committee covers a variety of aspects, the most important of which relate to the control exercised by the Laboratory over pharmaceutical preparations. Thus the Committee asks this Laboratory to perform studies or analyses to provide it with information on the identity, purity, dosage, stability and toxicity, in particular of new products, serums and vaccines.

Relationship of the Committee with pha:maceutical laboratories. In order to further scientific and technical progress in drug-related activities and enable the AMM Committee to play a constructive and not repressive role, close links have been established with the pharmaceutical laboratories. Within the Committee itself, the presence in an advisory capacity of a representative of the National Union of the Pharmaceutical Industry provides for concrete discussion of the problems under consideration. At the various stages of examination of a dossier, additional information may be collected from the pharmaceutical laboratories to enlighten the rapporteurs. Constructive exchanges of views have taken place between representatives of the laboratories and their experts and members of the AMM Committee and their rapporteurs in the framework of the appeal procedure, which warrants special sessions of the Committee.

The quality of the exchanges of views which have taken place urges the Committee to pursue and develop the policy of information and consultation which has been started with the Pharmaceutical Industry.

Decisions taken

The number of drug licenses is slowly and regularly increasing as shown in this table:

1978	1979	1980	1981
255	262	322	344

Such figures include all licenses given even for minor modification of the formula and for generic drugs.

The annual rate of license delivered for new drugs including new combinations is around 50 and the number of licenses for new active principles is around 10.

France has no " need clause "

Review of old products

The approach to this difficult problem by the Pharmacy Directorate and the Drug Licensing Committee is the following one.

Review of all old drugs licenses before 1991 is compulsory in agreement with the EEC regulation approved by the French Government.

The Pharmaceutical Industry should be informed in advance of the policy followed.

A working party with representatives of the Administration, the Drug Licensing Committee and the Pharmaceutical Industry was set up and has already met. Participants agreed on discussing this proposed scheme: Old drugs should fall into three categories:

I.   Drugs whose data in the dossier, or in the literature, offer adequate guarantees as far as safety and efficacy are concerned. An abridged dossier will be accepted. Rigid criteria to define category I were discussed with the Industry during the last year.

II.   Drugs whose dossier should be completed to agree with international standards. Requirement for each therapeutic class should be defined in the coming years within working parties including representatives from the Administration, from the Drug Scientific Committees and from the Pharmaceutical Industry.

III.   Drugs which will be removed from the market because data available on such drugs do not fulfil the new requirements for security and efficacy.

To avoid large discrepancies between various countries in relation to the decisions made by national Authorities, a thorough discussion of this delicate matter between representatives of all nations concerned, including industrialized and developing countries, should take place. This topic could be on the Agenda of the next ICDRA Conference.

Post Marketing Surveillance

A national drug monitoring network developed rapidly during the last five years. Regional Centers and a National Center dealing with post marketing surveillance collect the information on a drug's adverse effect coming from the practitioners, the hospitals and the specialised so called " anti-poison Centers ". Data are collected on a national basis and organized and analysed by computerized data processing.

Report of adverse reactions by the Drug Monitoring Board (Commission de Pharmacovigilance) may justify revision of the License with modification, for example, of indications and contra-indications. For safety reasons, the Board may propose to the Minister of Health withdrawal of a speciality from the market.

The effects of new drugs should be carefully monitored after the grant of the Drug License. Control of possible adverse effects should be reinforced. This alone can provide the guarantees of safety derived from an analysis of the results obtained when a new drug is widely prescribed by practitioners. Post marketing clinical trials mainly devoted to studying tolerance should be developed with the triple participation of the Ministry, the practitioners and the pharmaceutical laboratories.

Exportations and Importations of Drugs

Exportations

Two different situations are encountered:

a) *The drug is licensed in France.*

The guarantees offered to importing countries are those offered to the French community. Details of the drug license included in the data sheet are available giving all information on e.g. doses, indications, contra-indications... A certificate establishing that the drug is manufactured in agreement with the WHO good manufacturing pratice is delivered by the Ministry of Health. Further clinical or technical information relating to the product may be obtained directly from the Direction de la Pharmacie at the Ministry of Health.

b) *The drug is not licensed in France.*

According to the French law exportation of such drugs is possible but a special authorisation from the Ministry of Health is required to agree with article L. 603 of the Public Health Code. The certificate delivered should guarantee good manufacturing practice and the quality of the batches exported. Manufacturers are submitted to regular inspections.

These conditions apply mainly to old products. With few exceptions, the L. 603 article does not apply to new drugs exported but not marketed in France. In such circumstances the advice of the Drug Licensing Committee is requested.

Such a scheme should agree with the WHO objectives and offer the developing countries the quality assurance of imported drugs.

Importations

Three different conditions may justify importation of drugs in France under the control of the Minister of Health.

— Drugs required for clinical trials of new drugs under the responsibility of the Firm and of the Experts.

— Drugs, mainly orphan drugs, not marketed in France and required to treat specific cases. Authorisation of importation is given upon medical service.

— Drugs licensed in France, but manufactured in other countries. Special customs certificates, controlled by the Ministry of Health, are delivered. Certificates differ according to whether countries belong to the EEC or not.

This note is a short survey of the official regulatory control of pharmaceutical products in France and of the policy followed by the French Government to offer the world community all the guarantees it is entitled to demand in regard to drugs.

DRUG REGULATION IN THE FEDERAL REPUBLIC OF GERMANY

P. S. Schönhöfer

Institut für Arzneimittel Bundesgesundheitsamt, W. Germany

The legal basis for regulatory procedures was established by the Arzneimittelgesetz of 1976 (AMG) which introduced the evaluation of safety, efficacy and quality into the approval procedure. Prior legislation (AMG 1961) did not provide a legal basis for evaluation of safety, efficacy and quality.

Before clinical trials the data on basic toxicology and pharmacology have to be submitted to the Federal Health Office (BGA). However, these data are not evaluated by the office but rather retained for the purpose of a documentation in cases of drug related problems during clinical trials. Planned clinical trials have to be surveilled by the regional or local ethics committees formed by the hospital and regional medical associations. The responsibility for the supervision of the formal and legal conduct of the clinical trials rests with the Länder.

The process of licensing of new products prior to marketing involves a two phase system. In phase 1, decision is made as to approval or demand of further information from the applicant. The applicant is notified by a letter of deficiencies. This phase 1 has to be concluded within 4 months. In phase 2, decision is made on the new data submitted by the applicant. Within 3 months the final evaluation has to be made as to approval or rejection. The decision of the office is subject to a hearing of an advisory board (Kommission A) in cases of new drug entities. With " old " substances the decision rests with the office.

According to the AMG 1976 the review of old products on the national market has to be performed by 1990. Several activities of the evaluation procedure of old drugs are under consideration. A scheme has been proposed. However, regulatory activities in this respect have not yet started.

The control of manufacturing (GMP) is, according to our federal structure, under the responsibility of the Länder. Certificates for production as well as inspections are performed by the Länder. Federal activities are directed to joining the PIC agreement.

According to the federal structure, controls on distribution, warehousing and retail outlets rest with the Länder.

The Federal Health Office can propose limitation of the free sales to the Federal Ministry of Health (eg. prescription only, pharmacy only). The Federal Ministry of Health decides on these proposals after hearing an advisory committee. The control of the decisions is under the responsibility of the Länder.

Post-marketing surveillance is under the responsibility of the Federal Health Office. Monitoring of adverse drug reactions is performed by this office. The procedure for actions in cases of drug safety is documented in the " Stufenplan zur Abwehr von Arzneimittelrisiken ". This regulation determines the channels of information of the pharmaceutical industry, the Länder and the medical professions when drug problems arise. Measures to be taken include additions to the PPI, warning labels, restrictions of the indications as well as withdrawal of the product license.

Problems in pharmaceutical quality of a drug are handled by the Länder. The actions include temporary recall of the product from the market. There are about 2.000 quality related reports per year in the Federal Republic of Germany.

Certificates for the export of drug products as well as controls on exported products are under the responsibility of the Länder. Drugs for export have to fulfil the same approval procedure for safety, efficacy and quality as products on the national market.

Approvals are published in the Bundesanzeiger and several pharmaceutical journals (eg. Pharmazeutische Zeitung). In cases of safety decisions under drug monitoring of the Stufenplan, the data are again published in several journals and distributed to the newspaper for information of the public. Hearings on drug related problems of safety are performed in public.

SWEDISH DRUG CONTROL

K. Strandberg

Director Div. of Pharmacotherapeutics, National Board of Health and Welfare, Sweden

The principal aim of Swedish Drug Control is to guarantee citizens well-tested and well-manufactured drugs, i.e. efficacious drugs of high quality with adverse reactions that are not disproportionate to the intended effect.

Legislation

The first step towards the present legislation was taken in 1913, when it was defined which substances were to be regarded as drugs and thus only allowed to be sold by pharmacies. The main principles for accepting drugs were implemented in 1934. Thus it became compulsory to apply for registration at the National Board of Health and Welfare for products produced by the pharmaceutical industry and delivered to the pharmacies in the packages intended for the patients, and to prove the efficacy and safety of the products. This Pharmaceutical Speciality Decree was replaced by an updated Drug Ordinance in 1964 and minor legislative changes have subsequently been introduced.

According to present legislation a drug is defined as " any article intended for use, whether internally or externally, for the purpose of preventing, diagnosing, alleviating or curing disease or symptoms of disease in human beings or animals, or which is otherwise to be used as directed in the treatment of disease, injury, bodily defect or in connection with childbirth, all subject to the provision that the article has been put into finished, ready-to-use order for such purposes by means of formulation, dosage or dosage directions." There are several exemptions from the concept of a drug, e.g. blood intended for transfusion (but not immune sera or blood protein fractions), certain odontological and surgical preparations. Homeopathic agents are exempted, as well as ointments used for sores, inhalant oils, liniments and the like, which meet the criteria of composition and labelling prescribed by the drug regulatory agency. On the other hand the Drug Ordinance is operative in its entirety with respect to agents intended to produce contraceptive action after absorption, certain chemical substances such as amidopyrine, paracetamol, L-tryptophane etc., additive to infusion, injection or rinsing fluids or to blood for transfusion, medical aerosols, agents to combat overweight by accelerating the passage of food through the alimentary canal, dulling the sense of taste and otherwise suppressing the appetite, all subject to the provision that the agent has been put into ready-to-use order.

The Drug Ordinance also contains sections on manufacturing, importing and handling of drugs, as well as the trade. It states that the National Board of Health and Welfare has to continuously control registered pharmaceutical specialities and that the registration can be withdrawn if the drug is no longer found to meet the necessary standards. The registration can also be withdrawn if the advertising is grossly misleading.

One clause deals with inspection of drug manufacturing plants which makes it possible for the National Board of Health and Welfare to inspect places where drugs are produced or handled or places where preclinical investigations are performed.

Under the Official Secrets Act and the Civil Service Security Regulations, documents on matters relating to registration of pharmaceutical specialities, or to any investigations undertaken by the National Board of Health and Welfare into the manufacture of pharmaceutical specialities, may not be put at the disposal of the general public unless such information is considered to be in the interest of the public.

The view of these statutory rules is held to extend to entries in the archives of the National Board of Health and Welfare which includes applications submitted for registration, as well as to other documents which have been drawn up within the National Board of Health and Welfare in respect of these applications. The only decisions that are made generally public are those reached by the Board at registration meetings.

Since these rules were devised to protect the manufacturer, exemptions from them may be made if the manufacturer does not object.

Organization

The Department of Drugs, the Swedish drug regulatory agency, is one of five Departments within the National Board of Health and Welfare. It consists of an administrative section, a research and development section, the Drug Inspectorate and four divisions, i.e. the General Drug, Pharmaceutical, Pharmacological and Pharmacotherapeutic Division, evaluating and controlling pharmaceutical specialities and other drugs. The present staff consists of about 160 persons which include 22 M.D.s, 47 pharmacists, 34 technicians, 6 administrative officers, 32 clerks and 19 others.

The Department is assisted in its work by several advisory boards and by a number of permanent or *ad hoc* consultants from various fields of interest.

The Board of Drugs is composed largely of experts from various fields of medicine, veterinary medicine and pharmacy. The Board meets regularly and advises on the basis of comprehensive reports prepared by the Pharmaceutical, Pharmacological and Pharmacotherapeutic Divisions on approval for registration and withdrawal of registration of pharmaceutical specialities, both in the human and veterinary fields, and on new indications for already approved drugs.

The Adverse Drug Reaction Committee is similarly composed of experts from various fields of medicine and reviews information received through the Swedish Adverse Drug Reaction reporting system and other channels which have previously been processed by the Department. The Committee regularly informs Swedish physicians on more important matters in the field in an ADR bulletin.

The Drug Information Committee prepares reviews on pharmacological and clinical properties of various drug categories and arranges workshops to highlight current issues for the information of physicians.

There are also a Pharmacopoeia Committee and a Committee on Sterile Medical Devices.

The total annual budget amounts to about 38 million Swedish crowns for the fiscal year 1982/83. This cost is expected to be covered by fees for drug applications and annual fees for each registered speciality and also for the other groups of products which are supervised by the Department.

Approval of new drugs

Investigational new drugs (IND's). It is mandatory to give notification of clinical trials of new drugs in patients, as well as in healthy volunteers, and of approved drugs on new indications. Documentation must be submitted on composition, pharmacology and toxicology of the drug as well as of the design of the clinical trials. The data is scrutinized within the period of 2 weeks and supplementation may be requested. A proposal from the Department on new regulations concerning the supervising and performance of clinical trials is being considered by the government. If accepted, additional requirements on documentation and ethics will be introduced.

New drug applications (NDA's). Documentation on new drugs is evaluated by the Pharmaceutical, Pharmacological and Pharmacotherapeutic divisions. For assessment of clinical data consultants are often employed. Evaluation protocols are prepared and presented to the Advisory Board of Drugs. Decision on approval or rejection of the application is taken by the General Director of the National Board of Health and Welfare. The industry receives the evaluation reports prior to the Board meetings and may choose to withdraw the application when the evaluation is unfavourable. The evaluation protocols are confidential whereas decisions on registration and rejection of applications are official.

At present there is a backlog of 387 applications which, in fact, represents a favourable downward trend in comparison to previous years. To a large extent the backlog is the result of incomplete applications and manpower problems. In the fiscal year 1981/82, 183 pharmaceutical specialities were registered including 37 new chemical entities. 53 applications were withdrawn or rejected. No products are registered for export only.

Guidelines on the structure and contents of applications are available also in English and are revised on a regular basis.

Apart from clinical trials nonregistered drugs may be used in special patients granted permission on medical grounds by the Department of Drugs.

Control after registration

After registration

Pharmaceutical specialities are made available on prescription or over the counter in pharmacies alone. The following procedures of control apply.

Control during manufacture. The pharmaceutical industry follows the Pharmaceutical Inspection Convention and the Good Manufacturing Practices (GMP). Manufacturing units are inspected at least once a year by the drug inspectors of the Department. Sweden reciprocates inspection of industry within the European Free Trade Area (EFTA) and some other countries, e.g. Denmark, the United Kingdom, the United States of America and Canada.

Quality control. For newly registered drugs, examination of the packing material, chemical analyses, biopharmaceutical analyses and, when needed, bioassays are performed within one year. Test for pyrogens and sterility are included when considered necessary. Other drugs on the market are analysed at least every five years according to a priority scheme.

Safety control. To monitor adverse reactions to registered drugs as well as non-registered drugs used in clinical trials a spontaneous reporting system is operated by the Department. Physicians are encouraged to report fatal, serious and new adverse reactions and to feel free to report other adverse reactions as well. About 2,500 reports are received annually and they are all clinically evaluated. An advisory Adverse Drug Reaction (ADR) Committee assists in this work. In addition it is consulted in the entire field of adverse drug reactions. The material obtained by ADR reporting is accessible to the medical community and more important findings highlighted in the ADR bulletin. Industry does not have to report to the system but should inform the Department about all new adverse reactions encountered.

Advertising. Labelling on bottles and packages, data sheets and promotional materials are subjected to control in order to see that industry adheres to the terms of approval for the products. Package inserts are available for some products only, e.g. contraceptive drugs.

Drug consumption. Analyses are made of the trends of use of certain drugs, e.g. drugs with abuse risks, drugs showing an increasing incidence of adverse reactions, newly introduced drugs, drugs with unexpected rises in sales figures with regard to therapeutic areas, exceptionally expensive drugs etc. For this purpose, as well as to follow the impact of published recommendations or changes in licensing conditions, sales figures, prescription surveys, prescription-indication studies etc. are utilized. Sales figures are given in defined daily doses (DDD). Prescriptions are stored at the pharmacies for up to three years. Computerization of the prescription material is presently being introduced and will offer possibilites for record linkage approaches as to adverse reaction follow-ups.

Re-evaluation. Manufacturers are requested to report to the Department new findings of significance relating to the toxicology, pharmacology and clinical use of pharmaceutical specialities on the market. The Department also initiates re-evaluation of certain drug groups on its own. These activities can result in changes of licensing conditions including withdrawal of license, drug information activities etc.

The Swedish Drug Market

The number of pharmaceutical specialities including different strengths, formulations and combinations of about 800 substances on the Swedish market on January 1, 1982 totalled 2,600. In 1981, 143 pharmaceutical specialities, including 22 new chemical entities, were registered and 55 were withdrawn from the market by the manufacturers. About 40 percent of the products are of domestic origin. In 1979 the number of prescriptions was about 40 million and the total cost 2,422 million Swedish Crowns.

Drug information

The Department supplies physicians, pharmacists and medical students with information on efficacy, safety and costs of drugs available on the Swedish market. This is carried out by publishing reviews on drug groups and pharmacotherapeutic principles in various areas, adverse drug reaction bulletins, monographs on new drugs and information on interesting therapeutic findings, regulatory actions and other news within the field of drug control.

International cooperation

Sweden is aware of the benefit of international cooperation in order to decrease the regulatory workload. The Nordic Council of Medicines is an inter-nordic institution with the object to harmonize the legislation and the administration of practice in the field of drugs in the Nordic countries. Sweden has an agreement with the other, and the former European Free Trade Association (EFTA) countries, on mutual recognition of inspection in respect of the manufacture of pharmaceutical products. Sweden has

a similar but bilateral agreement also with the United States of America
and with Canada.   Sweden is a member of the EFTA committee working
on exchange of evaluation reports on pharmaceutical products (PER-scheme).
There is also exchange of information on NDA:s between Sweden and
Holland, the United Kingdom and the United States of America.   Sweden
participates in a number of WHO's activities, e.g. the intergovernmental
drug information circular, the certification scheme, adverse drug reaction
programme, the international information system on drugs (formerly the
Feasibility Scheme), and distribution of reference chemical substances.

It is Sweden's belief that many of the listed activities lend themselves
to more widespread collaboration and use than presently appreciated.
In particular the WHO certification Scheme, should be mentioned, the
WHO International information system on Drugs, participation in the
EFTA PER-scheme and the possible translation of Swedish drug informa-
tion material.

DRUG REGISTRATION AND DRUG CONTROL IN HUNGARY

I. Bayer

Director General of the National Institute of Pharmacy

REGULATORY MECHANISMS

Drug legislation

Governmental Acts, first of all the Health Act, decrees and regulations issued by the Ministry of Health (including the Hungarian Pharmacopoeia) and the authority given to the National Institute of Pharmacy in respect of all regulatory control measures, form the legal basis of drug control in Hungary.

The Hungarian Pharmacopoeia

The Hungarian Pharmacopoeia (6th edition) is the national standard of minimal requirements for drug quality. The fulfilment of its general standards as well as the purity and potency limits of the individual monographs is compulsory. The National Institute of Pharmacy has the responsibility to ensure the respect of the norms prescribed by the Hungarian Pharmacopoeia.

The National Institute of Pharmacy

The National Institute of Pharmacy is the national drug control agency in Hungary. Its main responsibilities are, as follows:
— selection of the materia medica,
— establishment of national criteria for drug safety and efficacy,
— control of the fulfilment of these criteria,
— management of the clinical pharmacological network,

— authorization for clinical trials,
— assurance of the scientific evaluation of new drugs (chemical, pharmaceutical, toxicological, pharmacological, clinical pharmacological and clinical data),
— drug registration,
— authorization for manufacture of pharmaceuticals,
— inspection of manufacturing plants,
— regulatory drug control,
— assurance of the objectivity of drug information,
— monitoring of adverse drug reactions.

Committee on Drug Administration and Clinical Pharmacology

This body is one of the standing committees of the Scientific Health Council, it plays a decisive part in the drug evaluation process, issuing guidelines for the preclinical, clinical pharmacological and clinical testing of new drugs, evaluating the results of these tests and trials and assessing the potential therapeutic value of new drugs.

Regulations on drug information

Advertisement of pharmaceuticals addressed to the great public is prohibited in Hungary. The text of labels and package inserts are prescribed by the National Institute of Pharmacy and the same Institute approves the text of leaflets, brochures and advertisements in medical and pharmaceutical periodicals, reaching health professionals exclusively.

Regulation of Good Manufacturing Practices

Hungary is a party of the international Pharmaceutical Inspection Convention (PIC) of the EFTA countries *. The Inspectorate of the National Institute of Pharmacy is in charge to regulate and control the respect of the provisions of the Convention. The GMP recommendations of the World Health Organization form the basis of this Convention.

THE DRUG SELECTION, EVALUATION AND REGISTRATION PROCESS

Selection of drugs

A large scale revision of pharmaceutical specialities was possible by the nationalization of the pharmaceutical industry: thousands of outdated and unnecessary preparations were withdrawn from the market and

---

* " Convention for the Mutual Recognition of Inspections in Respect of the Manufacture of Pharmaceutical Products ".

deleted from the Register. It is standpoint of principle that it is not in the interest of public health to increase the number of pharmaceutical preparations unlimitedly. In Hungary, at present, the National Institute of Pharmacy is authorized by the Ministry of Health, to decide, in the possession of the results of pharmacological, toxicological and clinical tests and after consultation with clinicians and experts of the Scientific Health Council, whether the marketing of a new drug is a health necessity or not. The aim is to serve the medical profession and the public with every new pharmaceutical preparation having real therapeutic value, and to avoid at the same time not only the circulation of medicaments of doubtful therapeutic value, but also of many different but equivalent medicaments and unnecessary drug combinations. Through this system the number of registered preparations has been kept under reasonable limits.

Preclinical requirements

All the details of preclinical requirements are regulated and prescribed by the national health authorities. Applications containing the data and results of tests requested by the regulations have to be filed by the National Institute of Pharmacy in the prescribed form. All data are scrutinized by the specialized staff of the Institute and evaluated by the Committee on Drug Administration and Clinical Pharmacology.

Clinical pharmacology

Clinical pharmacological tests are carried out by the specialized units of the Clinical Pharmacological Network. The results are evaluated by the Committee on Drug Administration and Clinical Pharmacology. In the light of the results decision is taken on the authorization for clinical trials.

Controlled clinical trials

Clinical trials are authorized by the National Institute of Pharmacy; the first investigators are designated by the Institute, the extension of clinical trials is granted after the evaluation of the first results by the Committee on Drug Administration and Clinical Pharmacology. The extension has to be requested by the manufacturer from the National Institute of Pharmacy; it is not allowed to conduct clinical trials with new, non-registered drugs without the authorization og the Institute.

Registration

The evaluation of the clinical results by the Committee on Drug Administration and Clinical Pharmacology and the formal approval of the therapeutic suitability of the drug by the National Institute of Pharmacy constitute a prerequisite for its registration. The manufacturer must submit his application for registration to the same Institute. The form of presentation of the data, proposed control methods, description of stability tests, etc. are prescribed in details by the Institute.

The registration of a pharmaceutical preparation includes the prescription of the text of the preparation's label and also the approval of the text of package insert.

ASSURANCE OF DRUG QUALITY

1. The direct control system

Departments for Quality Control in factories

The reorganization of the pharmaceutical industry after nationalization was very important not only in order to rationalize production, but it had a favourable influence upon quality. In contrast to smaller units (which disappeared) the seven big factories are adequately equipped with analytical, biological, microbiological and other special control laboratories. These laboratories are well staffed and equipped, and they are subordinated to the factory's Department for Quality Control, which is personally responsible, together with the director of the factory, for the quality of drugs. This responsibility not only implies that the quality of all drugs produced by the factory should meet the requirements of the Hungarian Pharmacopoeia and the norms established or approved by the National Institute of Pharmacy during the registration of the product, but in addition, that each of the substances and auxiliary materials delivered to the factory, as well as each batch produced by the factory, has to be submitted to the prescribed examinations.

Drug Distribution Enterprise's laboratory

There is only one drug wholesaler in Hungary, the Drug Distribution Enterprise (GYÓGYÉRT). All substances, domestic products as well as imported ones, being delivered to pharmacies, are subjected to the control of the laboratory of this Enterprise. The substances must meet pharmacopoeial requirements or the prescriptions of the National Institute of Pharmacy. Every case of quality defect is reported to the Institute for evaluation and decision taking.

Pharmaceutical inspectors; regional laboratories

The inspection of pharmacies falls within the responsibility of pharmaceutical inspectors trained by the National Institute of Pharmacy. They have to guide and supervise the professional activity of pharmacists. Preparations made in pharmacies are controlled by the pharmaceutical inspectors in their laboratories (there are 20 regional laboratories in the country) by taking random samples during pharmacy inspections.

Pharmaceutical inspectors play an important part in the control of registered pharmaceuticals. They take samples from each batch of registered preparations supplied to the county drug depots and subject them to formal and sensory testing. Any visual change (precipitation, colouration, etc.) observed has to be reported to the National Institute of Pharmacy. This drug quality monitoring system, consisting of more than 100.000 checks annually, is a valuable source of information for the Institute.

Pharmacies

Pharmacists are obliged to examine all substances supplied to the pharmacy for identity and to perform, in some cases, so-called informative (basic) tests, which are prescribed by the Hungarian Pharmacopoeia. It is important to keep in mind, that in Hungary pharmacists were freed of commercial interests, consequently their reports are fairly objective. Due to the fact, that every batch of the products delivered to pharmacies (registered preparations, active ingredients, auxiliary materials or galenical preparations) had been subjected to detailed controls in the factory, in the " Gyógyért " laboratory and/or in the regional laboratories, drug control activity in pharmacies is focused on the discovery of eventual labeling errors or incidental mix ups.

2. Direct control by the National Institute of Pharmacy

Inspections

On the spot inspections have always been the right of the national drug control agency, but the execution of regular plant and production inspections is a relatively new activity.

The " basic (overall) inspections " of the seven drug producing factories, performed at five year intervals, form the starting point for the systematic programme of the Inspectorate of the National Institute of Pharmacy. There are, in principle, six different forms of " individual " inspections, as follows:

— inspection as a prerequisite of authorization for drug production in a new plant;

— in connection with drug registration (inspection constituting an integral part of registration);

— investigation of suspected quality defects;

— inspections at the request of health authorities of a country importing drugs from Hungary (on the basis of bilateral or multilateral agreements or on occasional request);

— " follow-up " inspections;

— random inspections.

Inspection of the facilities and periodical control of the functioning of regional galenical laboratories where large volume parental solutions are produced belong also among the tasks of the National Institute of Pharmacy.

34 — I. Bayer

Experimental (laboratory) control

It is a matter of principle, that every application for registration must go through careful scrutiny and the establishment of quality requirements should constitute an integral part of this process. In our opinion this has to be executed by the staff of the national drug control agency. In the National Institute of Pharmacy laboratory work starts with the control of the draft specifications elaborated by the producer, containing detailed descriptions of the recommended methods of analysis and quality requirements as well as the findings of the manufacturer's laboratories using these methods. Manufacturers are obliged to submit draft specifications for each ingredient, carrier substance and the preparation together with the results of stability studies and other relevant information for quality control. Methods and data are equally examined in the Institute's laboratories and the establishment of " Quality Prescriptions " is the outcome of this activity. Quality Prescriptions constitute an integral part of registration.

3. Control by the National Institute of Pharmacy through surveillance and monitoring

The Institute's direct control activity is supplemented by two efficient control mechanisms: surveillance of the direct control system and a large-scale reporting and monitoring network.

Surveillance of the direct control system

Nothing can replace the reliability of professionals who are in charge of the day-by-day control in factories and the wholesaler's laboratory. The question of reliability is not a matter for speculation: close working relationship has been established between these laboratories and the Institute. The permanent person-to-person contact between the two staffs is the best method for the Institute to check the integrity and professional qualities of the staff members of the laboratories. The limited number of factories allows us to assure this form of surveillance.

Periodical inspections are carried out by the Institute in the districts; during these inspections a number of public and hospital pharmacies and the galenical laboratory of the district are examined. Through these inspections the Istitute is able to study and assess the functioning and efficiency of the local (regional) control mechanism.

Reporting and monitoring systems

The direct control system is the main source for drug defect monitoring. Reporting by " check points " is organized, as follows:
Cases of drug defects are reported directly to the National Institute of Pharmacy
by the Departments for Quality Control and
by the Drug Distribution Enterprise's laboratory.
Every case of suspected drug defect is reported to the Institute
by the regional pharmaceutical inspectors and
by the pharmacists.

This drug defect monitoring system is supplemented by the following sources of information:

Complaints in connection with the quality of exported drugs are directly reported to the Institute by Medimpex (the only exporter of drugs).

There are individual reports sent by physicians spontaneously or in connection with drug monitoring system for adverse drug reactions. Every report on adverse reaction is considered by the Institute as a potential drug defect warning, and in order to avoid mistakes and superfluous work, quality control precedes clinical pharmacological investigations.

There are reports by patients (or their family members), reaching the Institute usually via pharmacies.

4. Evaluation and decision taking

In order to ensure uniformity in decision taking, every case of quality defect is evaluated by the National Institute of Pharmacy, usually in close co-operation with the producer.

The decision-taking authority allows the Institute to fulfil its regulatory and balance-keeping role, in making use of one of the following actions:

— deletion of a product from the register (meaning its complete withdrawal from the market);

— stopping of production in a plant;

— removal of a batch from the market;

— sale authorization of a batch with minor quality defects;

— temporary exemption of a preparation from some pharmacopoeial requirements;

— modification of the quality requirements in the Hungarian Pharmacopoeia or Quality Prescriptions;

— introduction of new general measures in respect of production and its control, which are necessary to ensure quality;

— warning of the manufacturer (in the case of minor deficiencies).

DRUG USE SAFETY

Drug-registration and drug control are focused on the assurance of drug safety and efficacy, but even safety and efficacy do not constitute a self-aim; the basic issue is the quality of the drug therapy and the proper use of medicines.

1. Information services of the National Institute of Pharmacy

Publications

Every 2 or 3 years a " Vademecum " is published by the Institute containing all necessary information about the Hungarian materia medica (composition, indications, contraindications, doses, side-effects, interactions, etc.). This pocket-book is distributed to physicians and pharmacies free of charge.

A periodical is published by the Institute — also free of charge — containing information on new drugs, new indications, experiences of clinicians, warnings, etc.

Network of pharmacists specialized in drug information

There is a number of pharmacists working in pharmacies (their number is 50, at present) who were trained in the Institute in this specific field and who act in different parts of the country as "information centres" for physicians and pharmacists. They are independent from the pharmaceutical industry, consequently the lectures and information furnished by them are objective and completely free of commercial interests. They attend quarterly refresher courses.

2. Drug information by the pharmaceutical industry

It is an obligation of the pharmaceutical industry to send information material to every physician and pharmacy on every new drug at the moment of its marketing. The texts of these brochures should be submitted to the National Institute of Pharmacy. The Institute's authorization is compulsory also for the texts of advertisements to be published in medical or pharmaceutical periodicals.

3. Drug monitoring

In order to increase the detection of adverse drug reactions, a drug monitoring centre was established in Hungary. The mechanism follows WHO recommendations and practices. (The analysis of case reports is carried out by the specialized staff of the Clinical Pharmacological Network).

4. Drug utilization monitoring

In 1978, a new committee was created by the Ministry of Health: the National Committee on Drug Therapy.

The terms of reference of this committee are as follows:

— to undertake a nationwide study on drug utilization in general,

— to monitor patterns in selected fields of drug classes,

— to conduct comparative studies of national versus regional (local) prescribing trends,

— to compare national trends with international experiences.

INTERNATIONAL COOPERATION

World Health Organization

World Health Organization is United Nations specialized agency for worldwide public health questions, including the problems of drug control and Hungary is cooperating with and assisting WHO in its respective activity. Hungarian experts contribute substantially to the editing of the International Pharmacopoeia, including the development of analytical methods by the National Institute of Pharmacy. Hungarian experts are frequently requested by WHO as members of expert committees or consultative groups or as WHO consultants in developing countries. Every opportunity is seized by the Hungarian health authorities for the implementation of WHO recommendations and guidelines for drug quality assurance, monitoring of adverse drug reactions and side effects, human phases of the drug introduction process, Good Manufacturing Practices, etc.

The National Institute of Pharmacy has become WHO Collaborating Centre for Drug Information and Quality Assurance in 1982.

Council for Mutual Economic Assistance (CMEA)

Hungary has a great responsibility with the international coordination of the cooperation between Bulgaria, Cuba, Czechoslovakia, the German Democratic Republic, Hungary, Mongolia, Poland, the USSR and Vietnam in the field of " investigation, evaluation and standardization of pharmaceutical preparations " in the framework of CMEA's standing Health Commission. Hungarian experts take an active part in the development of Compendium Medicamentorum (quality specifications for the purposes of foreign trade between socialist countries) and maintain close working relationships with registration and control authorities of socialist countries.

Convention for the Mutual Recognition of Inspections in Respect of the Manufacture of Pharmaceutical Products (Pharmaceutical Inspection Convention - PIC)

It was already mentioned that Hungary is a Member of the Pharmaceutical Inspection Convention, developed by the European Free Trade Association (EFTA). The Convention is based on WHO's GMP guidelines, making compulsory the application of safe conditions in drug manufacture and the control of their respect through regular inspection by the competent national authority.

International responsibility of the Hungarian drug control authorities

Hungarian health authorities are aware of the international responsibilities of the registration and regulatory control agencies of drug exporting countries. In Hungary, there is no registration difference between exported drugs and pharmaceuticals in domestic use; fulfilment of the requirements of the Hungarian Pharmacopoeia and the Quality Prescriptions of the National Institute of Pharmacy is compulsory in every case. Hungarian authorities issue certificates on registered pharmaceutical preparations on the request of competent health authorities of importing countries. The fulfilment of this responsibility is largely facilitated by the active regulatory drug control system (with more than half a century traditions and experiences) and the central organization of the pharmaceutical industry and foreign trade.

REGULATORY DRUG CONTROL IN ITALY

V. Fattorusso

I take pleasure in submitting to this Conference some remarks on the drug regulatory control system in Italy. As in most producing and exporting countries, this system is rather complex and I have no time to to describe it. I should like, however, to draw the attention of the distinguished participants to a few aspects relevant to our discussions today.

1. Regulatory Control of Pharmaceutical Production: ensuring the quality of pharmaceutical products, both for domestic consumption and for export, is a responsibility shared by the Government and the manufacturers. In Italy, the Government's responsibility includes:

a) The licensing of drug manufacturers: authorizations for the manufacture of drugs (either galenicals or pharmaceutical specialties) are granted by the Ministry of Health after inspection of the plant in order to verify that the premises, the technical equipment and the internal quality assurance system are suitable for each medicinal specialty to be produced. The person responsible for the plant must be a graduate in chemistry or pharmacy and his name is listed in a national professional register. These provisions apply to the manufacture of all drugs, either for the domestic market or for export.

b) The supervision of drug production is carried out through periodical plant inspections by the Pharmaceutical Services of the Ministry of Health in accordance with the requirements of Good Manufacturing Practices issued in the Italian Pharmacopoeia. The authorization for drug production can be withdrawn if it is found that the manufacturer does not meet the conditions laid down in the authorization or the subsequent requirements issued by the Ministry of Health in the light of technological progress. The Italian Good Manufacturing Practices are consistent qith the WHO recommendations (resolution WHA 28.65); they apply both to products for the domestic market and to products manufactured only for export, in order to meet the needs of the importing country. Therefore, for all drug products manufactured in Italy, manufacturers are required to keep the same records. Italy is participating in the WHO Certification Scheme for pharmaceutical products moving in international commerce. In accordance with this Scheme, and upon request of the importing country, export certificates can be issued and information can be provided on the registration status and on the quality control of each exported product. Export certificates are delivered by the Pharmaceutical Services of the Ministry of Health only if it is found that the manufacturer complies with the Good Manufacturing Practices as recommended by the World Health Organization.

c) The supervision of the quality of products on the domestic market is carried out in the usual way by analytical controls of samples of marketed products in order to verify their conformity with the approved quality standards.

2. Registration of New Drugs: registration of new drug products is based on the assessment of their quality, safety and efficacy in the recommended uses. The requirements for preclinical testing and for clinical trials of new drugs are issued by the Ministry of Health in accordance with the EEC Directive No 75/318 which is well known to this audience. I should only like to mention that in Italy, since 1975, an application must be submitted to the Ministry of Health before undertaking clinical trials on new drugs. Drug legislation provides authority to the Ministry of Health to determine whether or not a drug product, for which a marketing authorization is requested, is an innovation, i.e. a drug which has not been tried on man or used for a particular clinical purpose. If the product is considered to be a " new " drug, the National Institute of Health (Istituto Superiore di Sanità) undertakes the evaluation of the preclinical data submitted by the manufacturer in order to determine the anticipated risk/benefit ratio; at the same time, a chemical control of the product is carried out. If appropriate, preliminary clinical trials (phase I) are then authorized.

It is worth mentioning that the evaluation of the risk/benefit ratio is carried out in two stages: a first evaluation of the preclinical data before the preliminary clinical trials (phase I) are undertaken, and a subsequent evaluation of the results of these preliminary trials before more extensive clinical trials (phase II) are authorized. Between these two stages, additional documentation may be requested from the applicant with regard to chronic toxicity, interactions having toxicological implications, foetus toxicity, effects on reproduction cycle, pharmacokinetics, carcinogenicity, etc.

The procedure for granting a marketing authorization for a new drug product is as follows: the data submitted by the applicant are reviewed and evaluated by a Committee of experts in pharmacology, pharmacy, clinical medicine, etc. and officials both from the Pharmaceutical Services of the Ministry of Health and from the National Institute of Health. The Committee, on the basis of its review of the submission, may decide either to approve the application or to send it back to the applicant requesting additional information. The Committee may also decide to reject the application, but the applicant can file an appeal to the High Health Council against this decision.

3. Review of Marketed Drugs: the aim of the review, undertaken since 1975 by the Ministry of Health, is to identify those products for which the marketing authorization needs revision for three main reasons:

a) The marketed product appears to be unsafe in the light of new knowledge acquired after registration through further toxicological studies and/or through reports on suspected adverse reactions.

b) The product is clearly out-dated by more modern products having better risk/benefit ratio. Manufacturers usually withdraw spontaneously such products.

c) The product has been authorized for therapeutic indications that are no longer supported by current scientific evidence.

With regard to products that appear unsafe, the withdrawal from the market can be decided very quickly by the Ministry of Health, as it was in the case of practolol in December 1974; this drug was withdrawn in Italy much earlier than in many other countries. In order to take timely and fully justified decisions, it is essential to have reciprocal consultations among regulatory agencies of different countries. This matter will be further discussed during this Conference.

The withdrawal of marketed products for lack of efficacy, or for a too low risk/benefit ratio, is a lengthy process that must allow the manufacturers to provide all available information in support of their own products, In spite of the lack of scientific evidence of efficacy, some products may be widely used and, therefore, are of great economic importance to the manufacturers. The review of already marketed products is being carried out by the Ministry of Health with the assistance of an Investigating Advisory Committee and the withdrawal of marketing authorizations is decided after having heard the advice of the High Health Council. The review started by the re-evaluation of products in some therapeutic categories in which there has been greater scientific progress in recent years. If it was found that an active ingredient became out-dated, all marketed products containing such an ingredient were identified by a computerized system and they were reviewed with regard to their therapeutic indications and to the other active ingredients contained in fixed combinations. Products containing out-dated ingredients may be withdrawn from the market or manufacturers may be requested to exclude the out-dated active ingredients from the fixed combinations or to modify the therapeutic indications. The review has been in progress over the past few years and about half of all registered medicinal products have been already re-evaluated. For 1,671 medicinal specialties, which did not comply with the current requirements, the procedure of withdrawal of the marketing authorization is in process.

The main reasons for undertaking the review of marketed products were:

a) The excessive number of products on the market as a direct consequence of the very peculiar situation of the Italian pharmaceutical industry after World War II and of the lack of patent protection.

b) The recent establishment of the National Health Service in Italy covering most of the pharmaceutical expenses of the whole population and calling for a more rational and economic use of drugs.

In accordance with the objectives of the national health and drug policies, the Ministry of Health decided in 1975 to carry out the revision of the marketing authorizations for old drugs aiming at reducing the number of marketed products through a systematic re-evaluation of their quality, safety, efficacy and labelling.

In order to facilitate the process of continuing evaluation of newly registered drugs, manufacturers are requested to provide information every six months to the Ministry of Health on the number of packages produced and sold and on all suspected adverse reactions recorded in the use of such products.

4. Controls on Advertising and Promotion: Article 13 of the Italian Law No 833 on the establishment of the National Health Service contains provisions for the control of drug advertising. The texts intended for the promotion of over-the-counter drugs to the public through the mass-media (press, radio, television) are under regulatory control by the Ministry of Health. Promotional material for prescription drugs are supervised by the Ministry in order to ensure that the therapeutic claims they contain are in accordance with the data submitted for the marketing authorization. Furthermore, the Ministry of Health issues a periodical Drug Information Bulletin which provides information to the prescribers on adverse reactions, contraindications and precautions to be taken in the use of drugs.

5. List of Drug Products Reimbursed by the National Healt Service: the inclusion or exclusion of products in this list is based not only on the assessment of quality, safety and efficacy at the time of registration, but also on economic criteria.

U. K. REGULATIONS

R. Williams

Administrative Head of Medicines Division
Department of Health and Social Security
London, England

It gives me great pleasure to respond to the invitation you have extended to me and to say a few words about the way in which the UK drug registration system bears upon the use of medicines which are or may be imported into other countries from the UK.

The Statutory Basis

By way of introduction, I should like to spend a few moments sketching in the general background to medicines regulation in the UK. Earlier piecemeal legislation was replaced in 1968 by the Medicines Act, a comprehensive measure requiring that before a medicine could be introduced to the British market, a UK regulatory authority had to be satisfied that it was safe, efficacious and of good quality, and further providing for, among other things, the control of clinical trials, manufacturing processes and standards, distribution, retail sale, and advertisements.

Responsibility for licensing decisions rests with the Health and Agriculture Ministers who formally constitute the Licensing Authority, and is exercised from day to day by permanent civil servants who analyse applications for consideration by independent expert committees who in turn advise the Licensing Authority. No application may be refused without reference to the appropriate Committee.

When the Medicines Act came into force in 1971, some 30,000 medicines already on sale in the UK were granted product licenses of right, and these are currently being reviewed in the same way as applications for new products. UK provisions for authorising the marketing of medicinal products, for the review, and for ensuring compliance with standards of good manufacturing practice are in accordance with criteria adopted by the members of the European Community.

Procedures for authorising clinical trials in the UK have recently been streamlined so as to enable pharmaceutical companies to decide more quickly and easily whether further development of a new medicine is worthwhile. The onus of responsibility for the conduct of clinical trials now rests mainly on the companies but the Licensing Authority exercises a monitoring function which may extend to prohibition of a trial where a safety hazard is identified.

Medicines Inspectors maintain the highest standards of manufacture for medicines sold or supplied in the UK, whether manufactured in the UK or elsewhere. They also inspect premises of Government health authorities (NHS) where pharmaceutical manufacture is carried on. Wholesale dealers' premises are also liable to inspection.

By virtue of decisions taken at the time product licenses are granted, medicines sold by retail must be sold through a pharmacy unless, in the case of certain simple remedies, authorised for sale in ordinary shops or supermarkets. Some medicines may only be sold through a pharmacy in accordance with a doctor's prescription.

Once marketed, surveillance of medicines in the UK is continued in 4 ways:

i. Through routine inspection of manufacture and wholesale dealing premises;

ii. At retail level by the UK professional body (PSGB) acting on behalf of the Licensing Authority;

iii. Through reports on adverse reactions submitted voluntarily to the Licensing Authority by family doctors and dentists. Their reports are followed up and warnings of possible dangers issued to practitioners where a serious adverse reaction is detected;

iv. A round-the-clock system is operated by the Licensing Authority to receive and interpret reports of suspected defective medicines, to issue any necessary warnings and to arrange — where necessary, and usually with the full cooperation of the company concerned — for withdrawal of a defective product from use. Licenses may be suspended or revoked when products or premises are found to constitute a serious health hazard.

When the Bill, which became the Medicines Act 1968, was before Parliament it contained a proposal that all medicinal products be subject to licensing controls whether for the home or export market. You may ask why in the end the Act included a provision postponing such controls in relation to exports.

A number of issues are involved in considering that apparently simple question. A purely practical one is that direct licensing control over exports would have very little effect unless adopted internationally by other exporting countries; a country wishing to import a medicine will turn to other sources if it cannot obtain it from a particular outlet.

More fundamentally, should control rest with the exporter or the importer? Each country has its own problems and its own needs. The UK Government take the view that its action should not deprive other Governments of the opportunity to decide for themselves what medicines should be made available to their people, particularly in consideration of climate, diet, culture, endemic diseases, and availability of medical services which may be quite different from those obtained in the UK. It is a corollary of this point of view that the expertise of the statutory bodies which advise on the marketing of medicines in the UK should be directed solely to evaluating the safety, quality and efficacy of those medicines in relation to conditions prevailing in the UK.

Information available to other Countries

That said, I should not like to leave you with the impression that decisions about the marketing of drugs in the UK are in any sense withheld from other regulatory authorities.

First I should mention an important exception to our general attitude towards licensing control of exports. This is in the field of biological products such as vaccines, sera, antigens and toxins, which are subject to licensing controls whether for home or export market, for largely historical reasons, having been so controlled for many years under the Therapeutic Substances Act, 1925. More fundamentally, it was thought desirable that the UK's long-established experience in the quality control of these medicinal products, containing substances the purity or potency of which cannot be adequately tested by chemical means, should continue to be available worldwide. Action taken to limit or prevent their sale in this country would automatically affect both home and export markets.

Second, information about UK marketing authorisation is made available to other regulatory authorities in a variety of ways. News of the granting of a UK marketing authorisation (product license) is published in the UK, normally at the time the product is placed on the market; this information is also furnished to other countries within the European Community. More widely, the UK fully supports the role of the World Health Organisation as a world-wide link between regulatory authorities, by participating in the scheme for certifying products moving in international commerce, and by making available information regarding new products, reports of adverse reactions, and the withdrawal of products from the market on grounds of safety. Furthermore, a great deal of information about particular products is to be found in the British National Formulary, the Data Sheet Compendium published by the UK Pharmaceutical Industry, the British Pharmacopoeia and the European Pharmacopoeia to which the UK contributes. All these publications are available to the regulatory authorities of other countries.

It may occasionally happen that the UK regulatory authority receives information about import/export trading in medicinal products, which appears to be of a fraudulent or seriously misleading character. In that case, in addition to investigating the involvement (if any) of individuals or companies in the UK, we would volunteer the information in our possession, on a confidential basis, to the other country (ies) concerned so that they could take whatever action they considered appropriate.

UK Export Certification

Thirdly, I should refer to a section of the Medicines Act 1968 which enables the UK Government to provide such certification as it considers appropriate for medicinal products being exported from the UK. The fact that we are currently issuing such certificates at a rate of over 14,000 a year is not only a tribute to the buoyant state of the Pharmaceutical Industry as an important contributor to the UK's trade balance, but also suggests strongly that many importing countries pay close attention to the licensing status of the products which the UK exports to them.

Where a product has a UK license, this fact is indicated in the export certificate documentation, and provides evidence of the safety, quality and efficacy of the product so far as the UK market is concerned whether the product has been manufactured in the UK or elsewhere. In the case of UK manufacture, the documents also certify that the product has been manufactured by a licensed manufacturer and that his premises, procedures, documentation etc. are all subject to inspection by members of the UK Medicines Inspectorate to ensure compliance with the Government's published guidance on Good Pharmaceutical Manufacturing Practice. Where the product has been manufactured outside the UK, the existence of a product license is itself a general indication that the manufacturer's facilities and practices are liable to inspection by the UK regulatory authority. I should mention at this point that UK wholesale dealers handling licensed medicinal products must themselves hold a license from the UK regulatory authority and are subject to inspection.

It is implicit in my opening remarks about leaving the onus of responsibility for import with the importing country that many exported products may be manufactured to a specification, or include a drug substance or combination of substances which are not required on the UK market. All UK manufacturers of medicinal products in the UK are required to be licensed, whether their products are intended for the home or overseas markets. Thus, "export only" products manufactured in the UK will be granted, on request, an export certificate which shows that they have been manufactured by a licensed manufacturer and are subject to inspection in the same way as the manufacturer of a UK licensed product.

Finally, for completeness, I deal with the "export-only" product which, although exported from the UK, has been manufactured elsewhere amd is not licensed in the UK. With few exceptions, the UK does not exercise direct control over medicinal products imported into the UK solely for the purposes of re-export. However you will appreciate from what I have said that we would not issue an export certificate in respect of such a product unless it had been granted a UK product license. Importing countries will however be aware that all EC manufacturers are required to conform to the standards of pharmaceutical manufacture laid down in the EC directives.

In conclusion, I hope I have demonstrated that UK regulatory authority makes available a good deal of information about the status of the medicinal products which it exports, to assist importing countries and regulatory authorities in exercising their own judgments about the suitability and acceptability of those products.

DRUG ASSESSMENT
IN NORTH AMERICA AND ASIA

DRUG CONTROLS IN AUSTRALIA

R.E. Wilson

Assistant Director-General Therapeutic Goods Branch
Department of Health, Australia

I feel that to put the procedures which I am about to outline into perspective, I should give you a short background on Australia.

We have a total population of approximately 15 million and governmentally the country is a Federation of 6 States and 2 Territories. (Recently the Northern Territory, previously administered by the Central or Federal Government, has established its own administration to deal with matters akin to those that are regarded as State responsibilities).

Each of the States has its own government which was intended to be responsible for matters internal to that State. A central government, which I shall refer to as the Australian Government, was intended to deal with matters affecting the nation as a whole. With this in mind, and without the knowledge of the therapeutic explosion to come some half century later, the founders divided the responsibility for controls over pharmaceuticals between the Australian and State Governments. The Australian Government control pharmaceuticals which are imported, exported or the subject of interstate trade, and also those for which it pays. The last-mentioned group includes about 90% of prescription drugs dispensed by pharmacies throughout Australia as part of the national health scheme or because they are prescribed for veterans.

The State Governments are responsible for controls over the local manufacture of pharmaceuticals as well as the sale and distribution of all pharmaceuticals within their boundaries. Thus, across the nation as a whole, the controls sometimes overlap.

Although there is some synthesis of drugs, or therapeutic substances as we refer to them legislatively, the majority of pharmaceuticals are imported, most often as raw materials. Virtually all new drugs, and certainly those which have got to the marketing stage, have so far been imported, at least in the first instance. Thus the Australian Government's responsibility for controls over importation of drugs has been the focus on which the country's principal drug evaluation system has evolved.

Regulatory controls over pharmaceuticals in Australia are exercised at two levels — through the Therapeutic Goods Act in relation to standards for established drugs and formulations thereof, and through provisions of the Customs (Prohibited Imports) Regulations concerning the quality, safety and efficacy of new drugs.

In terms of standards under the Therapeutic Goods Act, these are basically those of the British Pharmacopoeia/European Pharmacopoeia. The Act also allows for Australian standards to be written as wholly new standards or to over-ride or modify standards published in the official compendia. These may be specific standards, that is, applicable to a particular formulation or drug, or they may be general standards applicable to classes of goods such as injections, tablets etc.

We are concerned that our standards are appropriate, adequate and realistic. Thus, where there is need to draft or modify standards, initial procedures in Australia involve the utilisation of specific individuals with special expertise in areas such as pharmaceutics, biology, virology, biometrics etc. as members of the Therapeutic Goods Standards Committee. Subsequently, after circulation of these draft standards to interested organisations, including the pharmaceutical industry, and consideration of proposed amendments, the standards will normally be given further consideration by the Therapeutic Goods Advisory Committee where the wider implications of imposition of standards under the provisions of the Therapeutic Goods Act are exposed to scrutiny by sectional interests.

One of our government laboratories, the National Biological Standards Laboratory, undertakes random sampling of pharmaceutical products available on the Australian markett o establish compliance with satisfactory standards. Furthermore, an inspection unit comprising appropriately qualified and experienced officers is based at the Laboratory and undertakes periodic inspections of pharmaceutical manufacturers' facilities under the Australian code of Good Manufacturing Practice for therapeutic goods in collaboration with other appropriate personnel from the relevant State Health Authorities. I should add that the Australian code encompasses all the requirements recommended by *W.H.O.*

Certainly Australia supports the concept of the W.H.O. certification scheme and consequently the Department of Health is pleased to provide the appropriate documentation upon request.

Insofar as products intended exclusively for export are concerned, compliance with provisions of the code of Good Manufacturing Practice is assured if a certificate is issued, and a statement is included in that certificate if the product is manufactured for export only. Certificates are not issued for new drug entities if they have not been approved on the grounds of quality, safety and efficacy for marketing in Australia, despite the fact that the manufacturers' premises, facilities, procedures and staff are adequate in terms of the code of Good Manufacturing Practice. Many products proposed for W.H.O. export certification, however, are combination products, which would not meet the combination criteria applicable to products proposed for the Australian market, but contain established recognised ingredients. In these circumstances certification would be given as to compliance with the code of Good Manufacturing Practice, but an endorsement made to the effect that the product is for export only.

I should now give you some details of our new drug evaluation procedures. As you all well know, on virtually a world-wide basis, Thalidomide led to a complete re-think of control mechanisms at all levels of involvement — from basic research and development within industry and other institutions, to introduction or expansion of legislative controls by government. Since safety is a matter of relativity, for instance, one tolerates a considerably greater degree of toxicity or adverse effect from a drug found effective in treating a life-threatening disease than say a marginally more effective treatment for a minor illness. In the Australian situation at least, it was felt quite strongly that safety could not be divorced from efficacy. Accordingly, the Australian Drug Evaluation Committee was established by regulation under the then Therapeutic Substances Act and held its first meeting in July 1963. The Committee is comprised of 6-8 members, at least 4 of whom are medical practitioners, eminent in their field, and 2 of whom are pharmacologists or science graduates who have specialised in pharmaceutical science. No departmental officer may be a member of the Committee so that it provides advice to the Minister for Health which is totally independent.

Because of the specialised expertise required in some areas, the Committee has the power to establish sub-committees to provide expert advice. To date, sub-committees have been formed on adverse drug reactions, endocrinology, vaccines, parenteral nutrition, congenital abnormalities, anti-cancer drugs and drug information.

At the Government/Departmental level a new branch, the Therapeutic Goods Branch, was set up in the 60's within the Australian Department of Health to evaluate new drugs in particular, and to administer new controls introduced under amended customs legislation. These amendments to the customs (Prohibited Imports) regulations were fully implemented in 1970 with respect to all imported pharmaceuticals and allow detailed evaluation, where deemed necessary, of the quality, safety and efficacy of the products. In drafting the legislation we avoided use of the term 'new Drug'. Instead we regulated for a permit and licensing system. While seemingly complex in legal expression, the system is nicely simple in the control it exerts. In effect, all importations of therapeutic substances, or their subsequent disposal, must be approved by the Director-General of Health, our Chief Health Officer. This gives us the opportunity to evaluate 'old' as well as 'new' drugs when the need arises. We would, of course, like to be able to evaluate all the 'old' drugs imported into Australia but lack the resources to do so — at any rate on an individual product basis.

In essence, and bearing in mind my earlier comment that virtually all new drugs are imported into Australia, our permit and licensing system operates in the following way.

All imported biological products, that is, sera, toxoids, vaccines, toxins, antibiotics and glandular extracts, including their synthetic equivalents, whether for human or animal use, require the permission in writing of the Australian Director-General of Health to enter the country. This permission in writing usually takes the form of a TS6 permit which may be a continuing authority to import the substance for a period of about 2 years, or a limited authority confined to specific consignments. I should point out that veterinary biological products are not subjected to assessment by the Federal Department of Health in respect of safety and efficacy. (Quality only).

All other imported substances for therapeutic use require an authority from the Australian Director-General of Health, which may take one of two forms — either the importer requires a specific approval or permit for each therapeutic substance he imports, or he may be a licensed importer. A licensed importer may import any therapeutic substance under the provisions of this general TS10 license, but he may not dispose of it, if it is what we term a designated therapeutic substance, until he has the permission of the Director-General of Health. To fully understand the situation some explanation of ' licensed importer ' and ' designated therapeutic substance ' is necessary.

When the regulations were implemented in 1970, it was impractical to issue permits for all therapeutic substances already being imported on a regular basis. Thus licenses were devised to facilitate the continuing importation of these established substances by the large volume importers. The regulations therefore permit the Director-General to not approve an application for a license because the applicant is not a regular importer of therapeutic substances. Presently, there are 40 licensed importers. Other reasons for refusing an applicant a license concern his ability and willingness to furnish information that is necessary to establish the quality of the substances to be imported, the purpose for which they may be safely used, and whether they are properly packed and labelled.

Inadequate premises, equipment, records and qualifications of staff may also be reasons for refusing a license.

Now, what is, or how does, a substance become a Designated Therapeutic Substance? It can happen in one of two ways:

The Director-General may declare, in writing, a substance, or a group of substances, to be a Designated Therapeutic Substance in relation to one or more licensed importers. This mechanism is used when a problem occurs with a drug and the need to control its use becomes evident. To date the Director-General has declared only 8 substances to be Designated Therapeutic Substances in relation to all licensed importers.

The second way in which a substance becomes a Designated Therapeutic Substance is if it has not been imported by the licensed importer in the two years immediately preceding another importation of that substance. The reasoning behind this requirement is that if the substance was not being imported on a regular basis then its proposed use should be looked at. Not only does this mechanism control the use of new drugs but also of ' old ' drugs which have fallen into disuse for some reason. It is unusual for such ' old ' drugs to be revived for use in line with their former indications. However, sometimes they are proposed for completely new indications with new dosage regimes. The requirement thus prevents the automatic renewed use of these drugs. (Hydroxyzine — ' ATARAX ' (Pfizer) — initially a tranquilliser but revived for effective use in certain dermatological conditions).

A licensed importer must meet particular requirements concerning all importations of Designated Therapeutic Substances. These include giving 28 days notice in writing to the Director-General of his intention to import a substance. After the 28 days has elapsed he may go ahead and import the substance by means of his license without hearing from the Department. However, he must not dispose of it without the Director-General's approval and in accordance with the conditions laid down in that approval.

A licensed importer is also required to keep records relating to the handling of Designated Therapeutic Substances in books kept by him for that purpose. The books must be retained until the Director-General approves of their destruction. At any reasonable time of the day the importer may be required to produce the books for examination by an authorised officer.

I should add that exemptions may be granted in respect of non-biological therapeutic substances.

A list of exempt therapeutic substances is published in the Commonwealth Government Gazette from time to time. To date no specific substance, but four specified classes of substances, have been declared exempt therapeutic substances, namely: — Veterinary drugs, pesticides, laboratory chemicals and non-pharmaceutical industrial chemicals.

Although we have no definition of ' new ' drug, on an administrative basis we interpret it to mean, a new chemical entity, or an ' old ' chemical entity proposed for new indications or with a new dosage regimen.

All new drugs proposed for general marketing are fully evaluated in relation to their quality safety and efficacy. Drug sponsors are required to provide a submission compiled in accordance with a document, known as the NDF4, i.e. the 4th edition of our New Drug Form. The NDF4 contains detailed guidelines for the general marketing or clinical investigational use of a therapeutic substance. Broadly speaking it is divided into four sections. The first deals with chemistry, manufacturing, quality control and other quality aspects of both the raw material and final product.

The second section concerns animal and *in vitro* studies performed to establish the drug's pharmacology and toxicology. Effects on reproduction and teratogenic properties are also required. The sponsor must furnish all the evidence upon which it was decided that the drug was safe for human administration. The documentation must be presented with detail sufficient to allow independent evaluation.

The third section relates to studies in man. Information is mandatory on the various aspects of human pharmacology and must include reports of all clinical trials whether published or unpublished. We do not stipulate that trials have to be carried out in Australia. Reports of overseas trials are acceptable as long as they are well designed and documented.

The fourth section of the NDF4 is a summary of the entire submission. Normally three different evaluators are involved in critically assessing a submission. Each departmental evaluator has expertise in one of the areas corresponding to the first three sections of the NDF4.

I should explain that because of a number of factors, including the type of work involved, we have been unable in Australia to consistently recruit and retain our full establishment of evaluators, particularly clinical evaluators. Consequently, we do utilise experts external to the Department on a contractual basis to undertake new drug assessments on our behalf prior to final consideration by the A.D.E.C.

The summary is of special use to an evaluator in locating specific data in the submission which he may need to be aware of but which is outside his direct area of assessment. Proposed product information and other product literature are assessed by each of the evaluators insofar as these documents relate to his area of interest.

At this juncture I should state that both the Department and new drug sponsors have found it expedient to develop quite specific additional guidelines relating to some specific groups of products — slow release formulations, parenteral nutrients and non-steroidal anti-inflammatory agents are examples.

When a marketing submission is received it is put through an initial filter system. The filter is intended to identify applications which have not been correctly presented or are obviously deficient as regards the data presented. These are returned to the sponsor. Once through the filter, an application is referred to the Australian Drug Evaluation Committee for allocation of a priority rating for evaluation. Only drugs which may represent a significant therapeutic advance based on a concise statement submitted by the sponsor and the knowledge and expertise of A.D.E.C. members or, for other good reasons, may provide a therapeutic benefit to patients, are given priority rating. Evaluation of such drugs is commenced almost immediately. Applications not accorded a priority rating join the queue for evaluation in chronological order of receipt.

The three evalutations undertaken by the Department, that is of chemistry and quality control, of animal studies, and of studies in man, along with an appreciation of the most important aspects arising out of them, are subsequently examined by the Australian Drug Evaluation Committee. The Committee recommends on whether or not marketing approval should be granted, the indications to which marketing should be limited, and on the conditions which should be applied. Subsequent to marketing approval, the sponsor is required to furnish a report to the Department annually for 3 years, that is, it is subjected to a period of ' new ' drug status. The report contains details of the drug's distribution together with all relevant data subsequently generated. This includes all published and unpublished papers produced in the interim. It should be noted, however, that all reports of adverse reactions provided to the company should be notified to the Department immediately.

Clinical Trials

I would like to turn now to drugs for clinical investigational use. In Australia these tend to be Phase III in the main, but we would like to see earlier stage trials undertaken and would actively assist any drug sponsor who wished to do this.

Data submitted must be appropriate to the stage of development of the drug and to the proposed further studies. The investigators' brochure and protocols for every trial proposed must be submitted together with details of the qualifications and experience of the investigators and the facilities they intend to use. Only trials which are designed to yield useful, scientifically valid data are permitted. We have an agreement with the pharmaceutical industry and the medical profession that if a clinical trial submission is adequate, we will evaluate it and provide an answer to the application within 60 working days. It should be noted that no such undertaking applies to marketing applications. Once the evaluation has been completed and the application seems likely to be approved, a meeting is held between the 3 relevant evaluators and perhaps some other departmental personnel, the proposed trialists, and representatives, usually the medical director, of the drug sponsor. We have found this a valuable exercise in clarifying the requirements and enabling fruitful discussion of any particular problems that may be anticipated with particular trial applications. I think it would be true to say that of the investigators find these discussions quite educational and it is also an opportunity for us to gain greater co-operation than would otherwise be the case. We impose quite stringent conditions both ethical and legal, on trialists and sponsoring companies. Some of the more important of these are approval of the project by the Ethics Review Committee of the institution in which the trial is to be performed, informed patient consent, early reporting of adverse reactions and the furnishing of a detailed report on conclusion of the trial.

SALIENT FEATURES OF THE CANADIAN DRUG REGISTRATION PROCESS

I. Henderson

Director Bureau Human Prescription Drugs, Health Protection Branch
Health and Welfare Canada, Canada

The principle features inherent within the Canadian drug registration procedure are as follows:

1. An emphasis on timeliness of the regulatory process, predicated on a perceived need for more efficient and safer forms of pharmacotherapy.

2. The concept that only appropriately well-controlled preclinical and clinical trials are capable of producing non-biased results that can be analysed in terms of safety and efficacy, and that only clinical trials which are likely to produce meaningful scientific data are by definition ethical trials.

3. Only drugs of a satisfactory quality which have been demonstrated to be effective for claimed indications, and which are sufficiently safe to provide an acceptable benefit-to-risk ratio in the light of the nature of the illness, are " approved " for marketing. " Primum Non Nocere ". Cost benefit ratios are important to provincial Ministries of Health which are charged with the delivery health services.

4. No patient with a life or health-threatening illness who has failed to respond to standard therapy utilizing marketed drugs is denied access to an innovative therapeutic agent unless it can be clearly demonstrated that possible risks outweigh possible benefits (even if the likelihood of success seems remote).
    As will already be realized, the Canadian registration procedure involves itself with:

a) *Clinical Trial Submissions (Ind's)*

These concern the determination of scientific and medical acceptability of clinical trials.   In order to reach reasonable decisions, there is a comprehensive review of data relating to:

(1) manufacturing,

(ii) preclinical testing, sufficient to provide assurance of the safety of the drug for the experimental human subjects.

(iii) a satisfactory experimental design or " protocol ",

(iv) evidence of an adequate, ethical review of the proposed trial.

These aspects are covered in the Canadian Food and Drug Regulation C. 08.005.

b) *Prior to Marketing*

Before a market launch or before promotion of a new claim a submission (application) must satisfy the following exigencies. The determination of satisfactory drug quality; safety for patients who are likely to receive the drugs for short or long periods of time in different age groups, including those that have compromised organic functions; scientific and medical assessment of the therapeutic worth for the claimed indications (diagnoses).

The process is also applicable to General Drugs manufactured under compulsory licenses. Under these circumstances ' Bio-equivalence ' is an important feature. These aspects are covered by Canadian Food and Drug Regulations C. 08.002 and C. 08.003.

After marketing

The need for careful record keeping by the manufacturer. These include adverse drug reactions and may include specific post-marketing surveillance data as requested by the Health Protection Branch at the time of issuance of the Notice of Compliance. These aspects are covered in Canadian Food and Drug Regulation C. 08.007.

c) *An Emergency Drug Program*

This is operative 24 hours a day, 7 days a week to permit the sale of a non-marketed drug from a manufacturer to a Canadian physician for the emergency treatment of a patient under his/her personal care for whom standard therapy has been shown to be ineffective. Only drugs about which there is some evidence of possible benefit and about which there is some information (source, nature, human dose, etc.) are cleared for this purpose.

d) *Prevention of a Drug Lag*

The administration of the Health Protection Branch registration program results in a minimum of delays without jeopardizing the stringency of the Canadian approval process.

The time between receipt of an NDS (NDA) by the Health Protection Branch and issuance of a Notice of Compliance is variable, depending on many different factors, but the average total time for the years 1980 and 1981 was 320 days (10.6 months). The time of first response to industry after initial receipt of an NDS (NDA) is a statutory 120 days; the *actual* first response time (average) is almost exactly 180 days, remedied through a change in the nature and format of new drug submissions (NDA's). This hopefully will shorten the evaluation time about 30%. The new format which will come into effect in 1983 is exemplified by the following schematic diagram.

Pyramidal NDA:

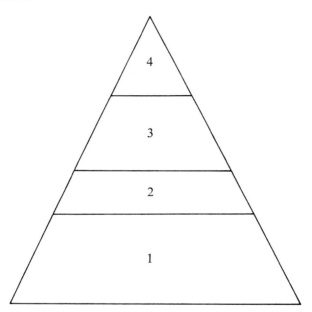

1. *Raw Data* (preclinical, clinical and manufacturing data). This will generally be in micro-format.

2. *Sectional Summaries* (pharmacy, toxicology, clinical studies) cross-referenced to raw data and to:

3. *Comprehensive Review* (Summary). A comprehensive assessment, and evaluation of the new drug, or appraisal of the acceptability of the evidence for a new claim for a marketed drug; cross-referenced to sectional summaries.

4. *Product Monograph.* This is the Canadian 'fact sheet' or 'package insert' that comprises full prescribing information for physicians plus sections on pharmacology, toxicology, kinetics and a bibliography. It is updated as necessary after marketing.

Each NDS (NDA) is reviewed by at least one pharmacist (initial screening), a chemist and manufacturing specialist, a biologist and a physician. A recommendation for acceptance or ' rejection ' is made by a senior staff member, who may recommend further data, elucidation, clarification, or new studies. If it is found to be satisfactory the manufacturer is issued a Notice of Compliance for the purpose of marketing, or in the case of IND's, for conduct of a clinical trial.

Old drug review in Canada has been progressings slowly, as resources become available. In situations where a health hazard may exist, specific reviews are undertaken, and decisions reached without delay regarding the advisability of continued marketing. Through a process such as this, it has been decided to disallow continuation of Strychnine, Bismuth, Arsenic, and Mercury in systemically absorbed drugs. A major review of OTC analgesics has just been completed, and a cough and cold remedy review will be commenced later this year.

With regard to Good Manufacturing Practices, a number of bilateral agreements exist between Canada and Sweden, Switzerland, the United Kingdom, the United States, and in a modified way, with France.

Advertising of drugs in Canada is controlled through a non-governmental organization — the Pharmaceutical Advertising Advisory Board — on which the Health Protection Branch has a seat. This Board pre-clears all advertising to health professionals — whether in journals, or by direct mailing. Without the PAAB stamp of approval, no journal will accept an advertisement. Advertising to the public on the electronic media (T.V.) is also subject to preclearance. The PAAB is financially self-sufficient through levies imposed on the advertisers.

Finally, may I emphasize that the Health Protection Branch is heavily science based, and that the backbone of our scientific capabilities is the Bureau of Drug Research, under the direction of our chairman Dr. Denys Cook. There are many unresolved scientific problems that manufacturers of new drugs are reluctant to tackle, or cannot tackle because of technological gaps in knowledge. These kinds of problems are passed by all components of the Drugs Directorate to Dr. Cook and his team of competent research scientists for solutions. Almost always, a resolution occurs, and this new knowledge is passed on to industry through open publication.

DRUGS REGISTRATION IN JAPAN

K. Shirota

Director Evaluation and Registration Div. Pharmaceutical Affairs Bureau
Ministry of Health and Welfare, Japan

1. Pharmaceutical Affairs Bureau

The major law which regulates drugs and drug industries is "Pharmaceutical Affairs Law", which was enforced in 1961 and amended largely in 1979. It covers approval of drugs, licensing of drug manufacturers and importers, labelling, advertisement, clinical trial, post-marketing surveillance, inspection, etc.

Pharmaceutical Affairs Bureau (PAB), Ministry of Health and Welfare, is the responsible organization to enforce this law excluding drugs for animals.

Chart. 1. Organization of PAB

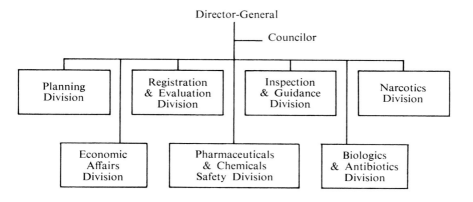

The organization is as shown in chart 1. 161 staff members are working in PAB (excluding regional narcotic control offices and laboratories) and the amount of budget in 1982 f.y. is 2,285 million yen (US $ 10 million Approximately).

2. License and Approval

Any person (company) who intends to manufacture (or import) drugs shall obtain a license for each manufacturing premise and approval for each drug. But some drugs listed in Japanese Pharmacopoeia (J.P. drugs) designated by the Minister of Health and Welfare are exempted from the examination for approval.

The drugs are classified by their status in license and approval as shown in chart 2.

Chart. 2. Classification of Drugs in License and Approval for Manufacture

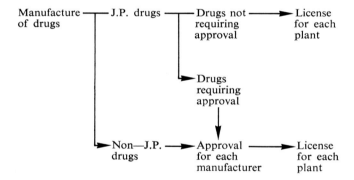

The flow of application for license and approval of drugs is as shown in chart 3.

Chart. 3. Flow of Application for License and Approval of Drugs

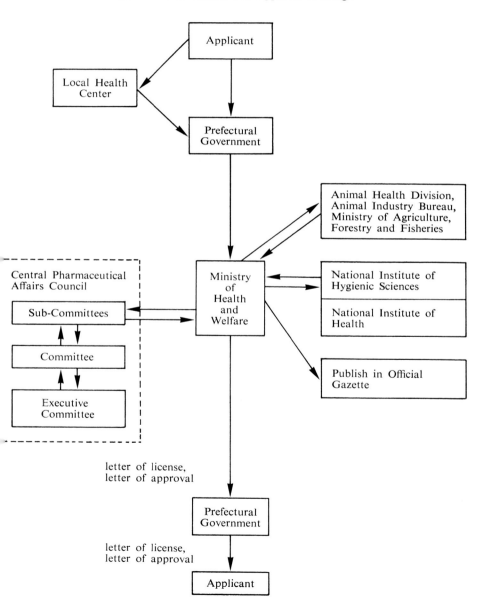

3. Central Pharmaceutical Affairs Council

Central Pharmaceutical Affairs Council (CPAC) was established under the provision of Pharmaceutical Affairs Law, as an advisory body for the Minister. It is an important organization for the implementation of the pharmaceutical administration, having functions to provide scientific advice and judgement as requested by the Minister.

The organization of CPAC is shown in chart 4. Each committee has several sub-committees.

For example, under Drug Committee which is engaged in examination for new drug approval, there are 7 sub-committees. These sub-committees are usually called for the meeting once or twice a month. Executive Committee and Drugs Committee hold the meeting usually 3 or 4 times a year.

Now 500 experts are appointed as members of CPAC. They are selected from various fields such as pharmacology, toxicology, medicine, statistics, pharmacy, law, etc.

Chart. 4. The organization of CPAC

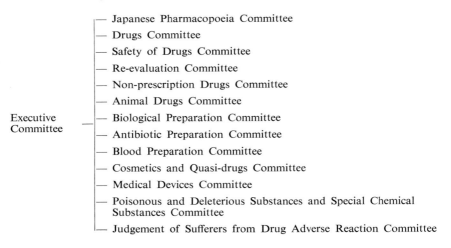

4. Approval of New Drugs

The drugs requiring approval are classified into prescription drugs and non-prescription drugs. The prescription drugs are those which are used by physicians or dentists under prescription or direction of such specialists. Non-prescription drugs are the drugs which have a mild action and are supposedly safe when used properly in due observance of the recommended dosage and administration; they are available to lay consumers over the counter of pharmacy and other drug retailers.

In some cases, it is difficult to classify drugs as prescription drugs or non-prescription drugs. The applicants are still required to classify the drug in the application form. The scope of drugs not to be approved as non-prescription drugs is specified in a PAB notification. The drugs containing new ingredients are, in principle, not approved as non-prescription drugs unless their safety is confirmed in clinical experience as prescription drugs. The standard for examination of prescription drugs, as a matter of course, is independent of that for examination of non-prescription drugs.

(1) *Classification of Prescription Drugs*

According to the PAB notification, prescription drugs are divided into the following eight classes in connection with the data required in the application for approval:

1) Drugs containing new active ingredient

2) New fixed combination drugs; they exclude multidigestive enzyme preparations, cataplasms with mild action, artificial tears, oral or tube-feeding nutritives and Chinese medicine formulations, when their novelty is denied after synthetic evaluation.

3) Drugs by a new route of administration

4) Drugs providing new indication.

5) Drugs in new forms; drugs which are different from already approved drugs, in principle, in dosage and administration as a result of pharmaceutical changes. For example, sustained-release preparation, though common in active ingredient(s), route of administration and indications.

6) Drugs in new dosage

7) Drugs in additional dosage form; they exclude drugs in 5) above.

8) Miscellaneous drugs.

(2) *Data on Drugs*

In the application for approval of drugs, data indicated in table 1 shall be submitted. The details of required data for each drug are specified in PAB Notification No. 698 according to the classification of drugs.

In application for approval of new drugs, for example, it is required to submit data on long-term storage test and severe condition test. For me-too drugs, on the other hand, it is required to submit data on acceleration test.

(3) *Examination of Drugs*

Procedures of the examination of drugs applied for approval are shown in chart 5. The application forms submitted to the Ministry of Health and Welfare through prefectural government are subject to preliminary examination in which they are classified in accordance with the above mentioned criteria and a plan is formed for discussion by the Central Pharmaceutical Affairs Council. Drugs classified due to the examination by CPAC committees and sub-committees are shown in table 2.

Table 1. Data required

Category of Data	Items
A. Data on origin, details of discovery, use in foreign countries, etc.	1. Data on origin and details of discovery 2. Data on use in foreign countries 3. Data on characteristics and comparison with other drugs
B. Data on physical and chemical properties, standards, test methods, etc.	1. Data on determination of structure 2. Data on physical and chemical properties, etc. 3. Data on standards and test methods
C. Data on stability	1. Data on long-term storage test 2. Data on severe-condition test 3. Data on acceleration test
D. Data on acute toxicity, subacute toxicity, chronic toxicity, teratogenicity and other toxicity	1. Data on acute toxicity 2. Data on subacute toxicity 3. Data on chronic toxicity 4. Data on influence on reproduction 5. Data on dependence 6. Data on antigenicity 7. Data on mutagenicity 8. Data on carcinogenicity 9. Data on local irritation
E. Data on pharmacological action	1. Data on test endorsing effectiveness 2. Data on general pharmacology
F. Data on absorption, distribution, metabolism and excretion	1. Data on absorption 2. Data on distribution 3. Data on metabolism 4. Data on excretion 5. Data on bioequivalence
G. Data on results of clinical trials	Data on results of clinical trials

Table 2. Drugs Classified by Examination by CPAC Committee

Classification	Committee		
	Sub-committee	Committee	Executive Committee
1. Drugs containing new active ingredient (excl. drugs in 3 and 10 of this table)	O	O	O
2. Drugs deemed to be examined carefully in view of indication, toxicity, adverse reaction, etc.	O	O	O
3. Drugs containing new active ingredient; salts, derivatives, substitutes, etc. of already approved drugs, which are pharmacologically related to them	O	O	□
4. New combination prescription drugs	O	O	□
5. Drugs in new route of administration	O	O	□
6. Drugs intended for providing evidently different indications	O	O	□
7. Drugs in new dosage intended for providing different mode of action or new indication by great increase in dosage	O	O	□
8. Drugs in new dosage form	O	O	□
9. Contents of examination of drugs for consultation other than those in 1 to 8 are decided on each occasion by committee chairman	O	O	O □
10. Extracorporeal diagnostic agents containing new active ingredient	O	□	★
11. Drugs providing new indication (excl. drugs in 6)	O	★	★
12. Drugs in new dosage (excl. drugs in 7)	O	★	★
13. Drugs common to already approved drugs in active ingredient, dosage and administration, and indication, and drugs within the scope of dosage and administration, and indications of already approved drugs	★	★	★
14. Non-prescription drugs regulated by approval standard, such as cold medicines, antipyretic-analgesics, insecticides, antitussive-expectorants, gastrointestinal drugs, etc.	★	★	★
15. Chinese medicine formulations effectiveness of which is well known	★	★	★
16. Drugs for change in specifications and test method which is scientifically well explained	★	★	★
17. Combination non-prescription drugs providing well established safety in view of their toxicity etc. and scientifically well-known effectiveness	★	★	★
18. Biological preparations providing well established safety and scientifically well-known effectiveness	★	★	★
19. Drugs with contents of application equivalent to those of drugs in 13 to 18	★	★	★

Chart 5. Procedures of Examination of Drugs for Approval

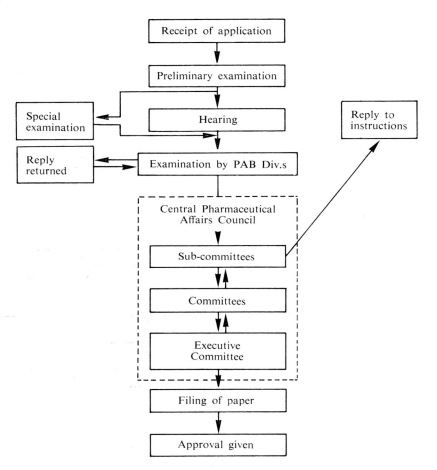

(4) New Drugs

The new drugs are generally defined as "the drugs having chemical structure, composition and indication which are not known before generally". According to the Pharmaceutical Affairs Law, a new drug is "a new indicated, by the Minister for Health and Welfare in Approving the manufacture of such a drug, as the drug evidently differs in ingredient(s), composition, dosage and administration, indication(s), etc. from the drug which has already been approved for its manufacture". A new drug should be regarded, in other words, as "the drug with a novelty which is to be required for post-approval investigation into the clinical use". The scope of new drugs, together in the data required in the application, is specified in PAB Notification.

Generally speaking, drugs classified into 1), 2) and/or 3) in the above classification are regarded as " New Drugs ". They are subject to studies of " Post-Marketing Surveillance " for 6 years after their approval, in principle, and the result is obliged to be reported to the Ministry every year.

The number of approved drugs which contain new ingredient(s) are shown in table 3. Imported drugs outnumber manufactured drugs.

Table 3. Number of Approved New Entities

	Manufacture	Import
1972	11	10
1973	20	12
1974	10	12
1975	12	18
1976	9	13
1977	13	17
1978	19	18
1979	11	24
1980	18	16
1981	25	36
Total	148	176

The average term from application to approval is shown in table 4.

Table 4. Term from Application to Approval (new entities)

1979	2 years and 4 months
1980	2 years and 10 months
1981	2 years and 4 months

5. Good Laboratory Practice Standard

PAB notified Good Laboratory Practice (GLP) Standard on March 31, 1982, in order to improve the reliability of the data attached to the new drug application. This Standard consists of 8 chapters, 29 articles.

The contents are as follows;

Chapter 1 General Provisions

Chapter 2 Personnel and Organization

Chapter 3 Facilities

Chapter 4 Equipment

Chapter 5 Testing Facilities Operation

Chapter 6 Test and Control Articles

Chapter 7 Protocol for and Conduct of a Study

Chapter 8 Reports and Records

It is similar to GLP regulation of U.S. Food and Drug Administration. It shall be applied to the studies which are initiated after April 1, 1983. For the studies which are under progress as of April 1, 1983, it shall be applied to the part of the studies conducted after April 1, 1983.

Japan's market for drugs is expanding year by year. Now, it is the second largest market in the world next to U.S. The annual production and export and import of drugs are shown in Tables 5 and 6.

Table 5. Annual Production of Drugs

(million yen)

Year	Production	Rx Drugs	Non-Rx Drugs
1976	2,162,436	1,799,418	363,018
1977	2,458,294	2,056,991	401,302
1978	2,793,878	2,350,579	443,299
1979	3,042,302	2,562,029	480,274
1980	3,482,177	2,978,437	503,740

Table 6.   Export and Import of Drugs

(million yen)

Year	Export	Import	Import Surplus
1976	63,672	173,043	109,371
1977	72,830	177,567	104,737
1978	68,337	184,039	115,702
1979	83,325	219.353	136,028
1980	93,901	262,363	168,462

In order to open our market to foreign companies more widely, the Japanese Government took several measures.   As one of these measures, new policy to accept data of studies which have been conducted in foreign countries was announced in PAB Notification dated March 31, 1982.

The points are as follows;

(1) Non-clinical data with regard to the safety conducted in foreign countries will be accepted if the studies have been conducted in conformity with GLP Standard of Japan or GLP regulation of other countries.

In order to enforce this policy, we ask the foreign government to issue a certificate which assures that the study has been conducted in conformity with GLP Standard.

(2) Animal test data other than those mentioned in (1) and long-term stability data conducted in foreign countries will be accepted if they are qualified for our standard.

(3) Phase 1 clinical trial data of studies conducted in foreign countries with the Japanese race will be accepted.

Japanese Government and people welcome effective and safe drugs which have been developed in foreign countries as well as in Japan.   And I hope my explanation as to the Japanese System is of some contribution to the international harmonization of drug regulation.

Thank you.

REGULATION OF HUMAN DRUGS IN THE UNITED STATES

J.A. Halperin

Deputy Director
Bureau of Drugs
Food and Drugs Administration USA

The Food and Drug Administration is responsible for every aspect of regulation of human drugs from early development through manufacture and marketing. This responsibility encompasses safety, efficacy and quality of the drug product as originally approved and during its continuing manufacture.

The legislative mandate derives from the Food, Drug and Cosmetic Act of 1938 which provided that a new drug required an approved new drug application for marketing. In 1938 the drug had to be shown to be safe for its intended use. In 1962 changes in the law provided (1) that no new drug could be studied in humans unless evidence was first presented to FDA that it was safe to initiate such studies (the investigational new drug (IND) provisions); (2) that FDA monitor these investigations in humans and require, among other things, that all research subjects give their informed consent; (3) that all drugs be manufactured according the Good Manufacturing Practices (GMP) regulations; and (4) that all new drugs be approved for effectiveness as well as safety.

New Drug Evaluation

FDA's involvement with new drug development begins when the drug's sponsor (usually the manufacturer or potential marketer) wants to test it in humans for its diagnostic or therapeutic potential. At that point, the molecule becomes a new drug and enters the regulatory system. The sponsor must submit a notice of claimed investigational exemption for a new drug (IND) before the drug may be administered to humans.

The IND must contain information about the identification, potency and chemistry of the molecule, the results of the pharmacology and toxicology studies in animals, a protocol or research plan for the proposed human trials, a commitment to obtain informed consent from the research subjects, and to adhere to the investigational new drug regulations. Once submitted, the sponsor must wait 30 days before initiating any studies under the IND to afford FDA an opportunity to review it for safety to assure that research subjects will be protected from unreasonable risk. Investigational studies are subject to review by Institutional Review Boards. FDA has recently promulgated new regulations covering the responsibilities of Institutional Review Boards.

Investigations in humans usually progress through three phases during which the necessary clinical evidence of the drug's safety and effectiveness for its proposed indications is accumulated. In the first phase the drug's absorption, distribution, metabolism, and excretion are studied. Controlled clinical investigations involving up to several hundred people with the disease or condition occur in Phase II. During Phase III, which may involve over 1000 people in both controlled and uncontrolled trials, the drug is subject to use by a larger number of investigators under conditions which are more like those under which it would be used once marketed.

During the investigational phases, FDA continues to receive reports of animal toxicology studies and reviews the protocols for human studies, but rarely sees the results of the human studies until they are submitted in the new drug application.

When the sponsor believes he has accumulated enough evidence of the drug's safety and effectiveness to permit its marketing, he submits a new drug application which contains full information on the manufacturing, specifications, packaging and method(s) of analysis of each of the dosage forms he intends to market; the results of any additional toxicology studies not already submitted in the IND stage, and full reports of all the clinical trials conducted. Under the law the FDA can approve the drug only if there is " substantial evidence " that the drug is effective; the clinical trials demonstrating effectiveness must be adequate and well controlled. In addition, the drug must be safe — that is, have risks and side effects which are acceptable in relation to the drug's benefits.

About 40% of all prescription drug products in the United States are combination products. The FDA will approve a combination drug product only if each active ingredient contributes to the effects claimed for the product. In a few special cases, the additional ingredient is added to: (1) enhance effectiveness of the drug by increasing potency or prolonging its effects; (2) improve safety of the drug by decreasing or reducing the severity of adverse effects, or (3) prevent abuse. The dosage of each component must be such that the combination is safe and effective for patients requiring such therapy.

The Agency uses advisory committees composed of experts in the particular drug class, toxicology, and epidemiology to assist in the evaluation of the evidence of safety and effectiveness so that it can make the most informed decision on the potential benefits and risks of the drug to determine whether it should be approved for the market.

The Agency approves about 15 to 25 new drug applications for new molecular entities each year. The basis for FDA's action is made available to the public and sent to drug regulatory agencies around the world. In addition, approximately 500 applications are approved each year for new salts and esters of already marketed chemicals, new formulations and dosage forms, new combinations, and duplicate products of older drugs made by generic manufacturers. Approximately 900 new molecules are in clinical trials under investigative new drug exemptions at the present time. Most of these new molecules are being studied by commercial sponsors who account for just under one-third of the more than 6000 active IND's; the remainder accounted for by individual physician INDs.

The 1962 requirement for adequate and well-controlled clinical trials revolutionized the quality of clinical trials and of drugs coming to the marketplace. In the nearly 20 years since enactment of those amendments, steady progress in science and medical knowledge has further changed the development, testing, and approval of new drugs.

This scientific and technological evolution has required continual updating of the regulatory process. A major revision of the regulations relating to new drugs is presently underway in the Agency. The current regulations governing investigational new drugs (IND), and new drug application (NDA) approval have been basically unchanged since they were promulgated in 1963. The impending revision is intended to modernize those regulations. In addition, the Agency will prepare new scientific guidelines, update existing ones, and make appropriate changes in the policies and procedures by which the applications are evaluated.

Review of Prescription Drug Advertising

The 1962 drug amendments also made prescription drug advertising subject to FDA regulation to assure that advertisements for drugs are not false or misleading. FDA regulations also require that advertising and labelling statements present a balanced picture of the advantageous compared with the adverse effects of drugs. FDA monitors prescription drug journal advertisements, promotional labelling, and promotional activities. It issues guidance materials and consults with industry to prevent problems from occurring or recurring. Regulation of over-the-counter drug advertising, is the responsibility of the Federal Trade Commission — an independent regulatory agency in the U.S. Government.

Post-Marketing Surveillance

Throughout the marketing life of a drug, FDA continues to monitor its performance through a comprehensive system of adverse reactions monitoring. The sponsor is obligated to report any information of adverse effects caused, or suspected of having been caused, by the drug. In addition, FDA maintains a voluntary reporting system by which physicians, pharmacists, and others may report adverse effects. The Agency also sponsors by contract an extensive system of postmarketing surveillance including registries for reports of adverse effects on the eyes, liver and skin, and programs to examine the use of hospital discharge and Federal and state health systems data to determine their usefulness in identifying adverse drug effects.

As new information about a drug's safety is obtained, it is incorporated into its labelling in order that prescribers have up to date information on the drug's safety and effectiveness. Where safety problems become so severe as to affect the benefit/risk ratio of the drug, the drug may be withdrawn from the market. The medical community is notified of major safety issues through FDA's *Drug Bulletin,* an intermittent publication sent free to more than 1,000,000 health professionals in the United States and to drug regulatory authorities of other countries.

Over-the-Counter Drugs

Over-the-counter (OTC) drugs have long been a vital part of our health care system. These drugs, which are available without prescription, provide symptomatic relief and treatment for minor conditions capable of self-diagnosis by the consumer without the need for scarce and costly medical services. An estimated 300,000 different OTC drug products are marketed in the United States.

In 1972 FDA instituted a review of the active ingredients in over-the-counter drug products. Because there are more than 700 active ingredients in OTC products, FDA decided that an evaluation by therapeutic classes of active drug ingredients rather than by individual drug products would be the best approach in determining safe and effective products. A series of expert advisory panels has reviewed tha active ingredients and proposed drug monographs for the various therapeutic classes. Upon completion of the program each monograph will establish marketing conditions and labelling for products containing each active ingredient that is generally recognized as safe and effective. In all, 17 panels met more than 500 times over a nine-year period and submitted 64 reports covering about 100 drug classes.

The panels classified the drug ingredients into one of three categories: Category I, generally recognized as safe and effective and not misbranded; Category II, not generally recognized as safe and effective or misbranded; Category III, insufficient data to permit final determination of safety and effectiveness. The panel reports and proposed monographs are published in the *Federal Register* for comment. The Agency reviews these comments and then prepares and publishes for comment a tentative final monograph (TFM) in which FDA states its position on the ingredients and labelling. Manufacturers of products containing Category III ingredients or claims have the opportunity to submit more information to substantiate their safety and effectiveness. A final monograph (FM) ends the process. It identifies those active ingredients and labelling claims which are generally recognized as safe and effective and which may be marketed in OTC drug products. All active ingredients and labelling claims not so recognized must be removed from the market.

Drug Quality Assurance

The Food and Drug Administration's responsibility does not end when a product is approved for the market. The Agency maintains continuing vigilance over the quality of drug products in the marketplace and the establishments that produce them. This activity is the combined effort of FDA's field forces in 22 district offices throughout the United States and the Bureau of Drugs' compliance and laboratory units. Compliance is accomplished through two primary programs: inspection of the establishments that manufacture, package and distribute drugs and surveillance of the products themselves to assure, through laboratory analysis, that they comply with applicable standards of quality.

The Food, Drug and Cosmetic Act requires that each facility that produces drugs be registered with the Agency and inspected for compliance with the current Good Manufacturing Practices (CGMP) Regulations at least once every two years. There are approximately 3,300 facilities subject to inspection. Each is inspected at least every two years; many of the larger ones are inspected more often. For example, almost 5,800 inspections were performed in 1980.

These inspections enable FDA personnel to determine if current Good Manufacturing Practice is being followed and, if not, to explain to the firm's management specifically what the problems are, and to report the findings in detail to the appropriate FDA District Office and the Bureau of Drugs. Non-compliance with the regulations may leave the firm and its products vulnerable to legal actions.

A CGMP inspection may be assigned routinely or for a specific purpose such as determining whether the firm has the necessary facilities, equipment and skills to manufacture a new drug for which it has applied for approval. The inspection also might be ordered to follow up on complaints.

An inspection may cover all facilities and processes in a plant or may be limited to a specific process or product. Inspections are usually unannounced, but upon arrival a written notice of inspection is given to the owner, operator or agent in charge. Before inspection the investigator will have become familiar with the operations of the firm and the products it manufactures and will conduct a short discussion with the firm's management to update any information at the start of the inspection.

Through a series of specific programs the FDA analyzes about 8,000 samples of drugs each year. The major effort is the Quality Assurance of Selected Marketed Drugs Program in which certain drugs are selected on the basis of medical importance, market share, number of products in the marketplace, and previous compliance record. Other programs focus on specific drug products such as antibiotics, radiopharmaceuticals, or sterile injectables. When unacceptable deviations are found there is a double check to see if there is truly a problem with the product rather than with the method of analysis. The manufacturer is first asked to investigate and, if necessary, to recall the drug product on a voluntary basis. If this does not solve the problem the product may be seized and removed from the market by court order.

These programs generally have been very successful and the vast majority of drugs in the marketplace are manufactured in the facilities which are in compliance with the CGMPs and which themselves meet applicable standards of quality. Through the use of compliance profiles, FDA can determine which manufacturers normally have no problems or only minor or random ones and which have histories of repeated defects in particular processes.

The Agency is applying the same analytical techniques to the results of the laboratory tests of the thousands of samples taken over the past few years to determine which dosage forms and products have histories of manufacturing defects so that special attention can be given them.

Imports and Exports

The United States imports a considerable amount of drugs, although mostly in the form of bulk substances. The requirements for imported materials are the same as those for domestic products. New drugs which require approved new drug applications for marketing must have these applications approved before they can be imported. Drugs which do not require NDAs for marketing may be imported subject to detention when they pass through customs. FDA inspectors visit drug manufacturing establishments around the world before their products can be imported into the United States. Copies of these inspection reports are available to the regulatory agencies in the home countries and are available to the public under the Freedom of Information Act.

Exports are subject to rather strict statutory requirements. A new drug product or new drug substance may not be exported unless it is the subject of an approved new drug application, or, if the drug is for investigational use, it must be so labelled, and arrangements must be made through our State Department or the foreign consignee must have a U.S. IND. There is a statutory provision for the export of materials that do not meet our standards of quality or labelling, but this provision is not applicable to new drugs and can be used only if there is written acknowledgement from the receiving government that the drug meets the standards of the country to which it is being shipped; meets the specifications of the foreign purchaser; is labelled that it is intended for export; and is not offered for sale in domestic commerce. A separate provision permits export of uncertified antibiotics. There recently has been some interest in relaxing the prohibition against the exportation of new drugs which have not been approved in the United States because of the perceived need for certain drugs in other countries and the capacity of the American pharmaceutical industry to supply them. Although authority to export unapproved products exists in our medical device laws, it is uncertain, at best, whether the provisions will be enacted into the drug laws. There is strong opposition to allowing drug firms to export products from the U.S. which have not been shown to be safe and effective for use there.

Current Events

1. *Antibiotic Certification*

Since the early 1940s antibiotics in the United States have been subject to batch certification for quality before approval for marketing. Antibiotics represented a new technology subject to considerable variation and succeeding batches differed in purity and potency. Progress in the manufacturing technology since that time has resulted in antibiotics that now are manufactured with the same assurance of quality as non-antibiotic drugs. Batch certification now has become unnecessary to assure quality. Food and drug administration data show that over the past ten years the number of batches rejected for not meeting standards each year has continually declined to where the defect rate was 0.16% last year. About 20,000 batches are analyzed each year. The Food and Drug Administration plans to publish shortly, a proposal to exempt all remaining antibiotic dosage forms and bulks from the certification requirements; topical and vaginal antibiotic drug products were exempted in October 1981.

After analyzing comments on the proposal we shall publish a final order which will likely end the antibiotic certification program by September 30, 1982. Antibiotics will then be subject to the same kind of laboratory testing as other drug products enjoy. We do not expect this will result in any decline in the quality of antibiotic products in the marketplace.

2. *Post 1962 ANDAs*

The abbreviated new drug application is the vehicle by which industry can apply for marketing approval for generic products of drugs originally approved on the basis of safety only between 1938 and 1962. Following enactment of the 1962 amendments, these drugs were reviewed for effectiveness under the Agency's Drug Efficacy Study and those found effective were permitted to submit abbreviated applications to market generic versions. Abbreviated new drug applications are permitted only for drugs where the Agency has made a finding of the safety and effectiveness of the drug entity. The applicant need submit only information on bio-availability and manufacturing for the product he intends to market. The generic drug industry in the United States has been anxious to have the use of the abbreviated new drug application extended to drugs approved after 1962 and the Agency is considering a proposal to open the post-62 new drugs to the use of the ANDA. This action may be opposed by the innovator sector of the drug industry that sees it as a threat against marketing exclusivity. The innovator industry has appealed to the Administration and Congress to enact patent restoration legislation to restore to the effective patent life of the drug the time the drug is subject to the pre-approval requirements of the drug regulatory system. The post-62 ANDA regulatory proposal will be considered by the Commissioner shortly.

3. *Regulatory Flexibility — Retrospective Review*

The Regulatory Flexibility Act of 1979 requires all Government Agencies
to review their existing regulations over a 10-year period to reconfirm
their need, to eliminate unnecessary regulations and to bring the regulations
up to date with modern requirements. The project to examine these regulations is called the " Retrospective Review ". There gulations of the Food
and Drug Administration now include several thousand individual regulations in nine volumes occupying about 10 inches of shelf space. The
regulations applicable to human drugs account for about 20 % of the total.
The Bureau of Drugs is starting its retrospective review with evaluations
of the IND and NDA regulations, the antibiotic certification regulations,
the patent package insert regulations (which we have proposed to repeal),
the good manufacturing practice regulations, and certain reporting requirements under the Narcotic Addiction Treatment Act of 1974 regarding the
use of methadone for addiction maintenance therapy. As we complete revision of these regulations we shall move on to others.

4. *Reorganization*

Last, but certainly not least, when the Commissioner announced the
appointment of Dr. Harry M. Meyer, Jr. as director of the Bureau of Drugs,
he announced simultaneously that the Bureau of Drugs and the Bureau of
Biologics, which Dr. Meyer has headed for ten years, will be merged into
a combined organization under Dr. Meyer's leadership. We expect the new
organizational structure will be announced shortly.

Although the name and the organizational table may change, our commitment to the principle that the public must have access to an adequate
supply of safe, effective, high quality, properly labelled drugs at compe-
titive prices shall not waiver.

SMALL REGULATORY AGENCIES

REGISTRATION
OF PHARMACEUTICAL SPECIALITIES IN ICELAND

G. Kristinsdottir

Committee on Pharmaceuticals, Iceland

Registration of pharmaceutical specialities became compulsory by law in Iceland in 1963 and henceforth they had to be approved by health authorities before they could be marketed.

A drug is defined in the Pharmaceuticals Act as any kind of substance or chemical compound, intended to cure, alleviate or prevent diseases or symptoms in human or animals, and substances used for diagnostic purposes including radioactive substances for use in or on human bodies or animals. Substances used in general or local anaesthesia are counted as drugs, also substances in approved pharmaceutical dosage forms intended as contraceptives or to increase human or animal fertility. Exempted from the drug definition are disinfectants and some oral vitamin preparations.

A pharmaceutical speciality is defined by law as a fully prepared or practically ready to use pharmaceutical, manufactured by an approved manufacturer in accordance with a standardized formula and given a special name or, in certain instances, a synonyme. Pharmaceutical specialities must be sold or delivered in the original containers and may not be sold, delivered or imported unless they are registered in a Register of Pharmaceutical Specialities.

However, the Ministry of Health can, if recommended by the Committee on Pharmaceuticals and the Chief Medical Officer, given exemptions to import unregistered drugs. Drugs imported under such a licence are always subject to prescription.

The Committee on Pharmaceuticals was established by law in 1963 as an advisory body to the health authorities and the Committee became responsible for a detailed evaluation of all applications for registration of pharmaceutical specialities.

Eight persons sit on the Committee on Pharmaceuticals:

Tab. I. Committee on Pharmaceuticals in Iceland

---

1. A specialist in pharmacology or clinical pharmacology.

2. A pharmacist being specialist in medicinal chemistry.

3. A specialist in internal medicine.

4. An apothecary nominated by the Icelandic Apothecaries Association.

5. A pharmacist nominated by the Icelandic Pharmacists Association.

6. A physician nominated by the Icelandic Medical Association and he shall be a general practitioner or a practicing specialist.

7. The Chief Veterinary Officer.

8. A district Veterinary Officer, nominated by the Icelandic Veterinary Association.

All the members of the Committee are full time professionals and their work on the Committee is therefore additional to their regular work. The office staff consists of one professional and one clerk.

The Committee on Pharmaceuticals is divided into two groups. The three first mentioned Committee members handle matters concerning registration of pharmaceutical specialities and withdrawal of registration. The Chief Veterinary Officer and the district Veterinary Officer are acting Committee members only when applications on veterinary products are on the agenda and other matters relating to veterinary practice. None of these members may have any interest in the sale, importation or production of pharmaceuticals.

A registration of a pharmaceutical speciality is applied for to the Ministry of Health and Social Security on a special form. Each application covers only one pharmaceutical speciality in a single dispensing form. A registration fee US $ 85 must be paid and half of this amount for each additional dispensing form of the same speciality. The registration fee for domestic applications is half of the normal fee, a decision made to promote domestic pharmaceutical industry.

An application for registration of a new drug is assessed by the Committee on Pharmaceuticals. The secretary gives the application file a preliminary examination to check whether there are major deficiencies in documentation. In such cases a letter is sent to the manufacturer or his agency, requesting supplementary information before the examination of the application file starts. Further deficiencies of documentation may also be discovered during the evaluation process and requests for supplementary data are then made. Having evaluated the file the Committee members write evaluation reports, a pharmaceutical chemical report and a pharmacological clinical report. During this penetration of the application the Committee as a whole may find it necessary to consult medical specialists in the various fields of medicine. The Committee issued in 1980 detailed guidelines for such external assessors.

Table II. Proposals of registration of a pharmaceutical speciality.

Name of the pharmaceutical speciality

Manufacturer — Agent in Iceland

Dispensing form and strength

Active ingredients

Stability

Storage conditions

Special registration stipulations

Proposed date of registration

The Drug Inspectorate's price — evaluation

Indications, accepted for the drug

Contraindications

Side — effects

Interactions

Toxic effects

Warning

Dosage for adults

Dosage for children

Special inscriptions

On prescription only or OTC

Reimboursment by the National Health Service

Classification in the ATC — system

Package

Price

Colouring dyes

Special labelling for OTC — drugs.

It should be mentioned here, that the secretariat receives evaluation reports from the other Nordic countries. These are frequently used if they are available for a drug currently under evaluation. However, the final decision on registration is not always identical in the Nordic countries.

When evaluation reports are ready the Drug Inspectorate is asked to assess the price of the drug. Usually the basis for comparision is the price of identical or similar drugs on the Icelandic market or on the market in the other Nordic countries.

The conclusion on whether to recommend registration or not is taken during meetings by the Committee on Pharmaceuticals, which are usually held once or twice a month. The Committee's recommendations are then sent to the Pharmaceutical Division at the Ministry of Health and Social Security which officially grants the registration or informs the applicant of rejection.

When an application is rejected the applicant is informed about the main reason. In the Pharmaceuticals Act there is no clause for the manufacturer to appeal against a rejection of registration of a drug. On the other hand it is quite common that representatives of foreign manufacturers ask for more detailed explanation of such a rejection, either direct from the Committee or through the Ministry. Furthermore is it common that the Committee receives renewed applications for drugs already rejected with a supplementary documentation.

The recommendation for registration is sent to the Ministry of Health and contains the following:

Name of the pharmaceutical speciality, manufacturer, agent in Iceland, dispensing form and strength, active ingredients, stability, storage conditions, special registration stipulations, proposed date of registration, the Drug Inspectorate's price-evaluation. Accepted indications for the drug, contraindications, side-effects, interactions, toxic effects, warning, dosage for adults, dosage for children, special inscription, on prescription only or OTC, reimbursment by the National Health Service, the place in the ATC-classification system which is based on the EPhMRA-system (European-Pharmaceutical Market Research Association), the package and price. Colouring dyes, special labelling for OCT-drugs.

This information is also to be found in the Register of Pharmaceutical Specialities in Iceland, which is prepared by the Committee on Pharmaceuticals and published each year by the Ministry of Health. A supplement is issued quarterly containing information on recently registered drugs and those that have been withdrawn from the market during the quarter.

A registration of a pharmaceutical speciality is granted for a period of 5 years. The manufacturer does not have to file an application for renewal of registration. According to the Pharmaceuticals Act the Committee on Pharmaceuticals shall every 5 years assess whether the premises still hold good for the registration of pharmaceutical specialities. The Committee can ask for further information about registered drugs at any time and the manufacturers are obliged to grant the Committee any information on registered pharmaceuticals.

Registration of a pharmaceutical speciality can be restricted to specialty departments, hospitals and/or by prescription of specialists in a certain speciality of medicine. If the Committee considers a drug important or promising it allows registration for 2 years even though the clinical use or possible side-effects are not considered documentated sufficiently. In such an instance the manufacturer must apply again for registration following the two years trial period.

The Committee on Pharmaceuticals in Iceland has shared with other Nordic countries the evaluation of applications for some new drugs. This will be presented here during the conference by a representative of the Nordic Council on Medicines.

To give you an idea of the number of applications for registration of pharmaceutical specialities in Iceland the last 5 years and the results of the evaluation I would like to present the following tables:

Table III. Number of applications for registration of pharmaceutical specialities

Year	Number of applications not finally assessed January 1st	Number of new applications received during the year	Number of applications taken into final assessment during the year
1977	130	123	136
1978	117	172	109
1979	180	135	115
1980	200	152	82
1981	237	135	202
1982	170		

Tab. III shows the number of applications which have not been finally assessed the 1st of January last 5 years, how many new applications were received during the year and the number of applications taken into final assessment during the year. The relatively high number of applications finally assessed in 1981 can be explained by the fact that the registration of domestic specialities increased significantly that year.

G. Kristinsdottir

Table IV. Results of assessment in 5 years and average time for handling in months

Year	Number of applications taken into final assessment during the year	Approved	Rejected	Number of applications withdrawn by the manufacturer	Average time for handling	Longest time	Shortest time
1977	136	92	43	1	11,1	38	1
1978	109	90	16	3	11,0	30	1
1979	115	84	30	1	14,0	39	1
1980	82	71	11	0	16,0	34	1
1981	208	160	42	6	18,4	44	0

Tab. IV shows the results of assessments during the last 5 years and the average time of handling.

Table V. Applications approved in 1981.

Comments	Number of applications	Number of drugs	Number of dispensing forms and strengths
New substances	26	16	26
New combinations	12	12	13
Similar substances and combinations previously registered	73	48	73
New dispensing forms	28	22	27
New indications	4	4	4
Prolonged registration	7	4	7
Modifications in already registered drugs	10	9	10
Total	160	115	160

Tab. V shows the division among approved drugs in 1981 between various categories, namely, new substances, new combinations, similar substances and combinations previously registered, new dispensing forms, new indications, prolonged registration, modifications in already registered drugs.

Table VI. Applications rejected in 1981.

Comments	Number of applications	Number of drugs	Number of dispensing forms and strengths
New substances	21	14	23
New combinations	4	4	4
Similar substances and combinations previously registered	11	7	11
New dispensing forms	4	4	4
New indications	2	2	2
Total	42	31	44

Tab. VI shows similarly the categories of drugs which were rejected in 1981, namely new substances, new combinations, similar substances and combinations previously registered, new dispensing forms and new indications.

Table VII. 42 registration applications rejected in 1981.

Main reason for rejection	Number of applications
Pharmaceutical-chemical documentation unsatisfactory	1
Bioavailability data unsatisfactory	8
Clinical documentation unsatisfactory	6
Clinical documentation unsatisfactory + other reasons	11
No benefits proven	7
Side-effects	1
Price	2
Azo-dyes	3
Other reasons	3
Total	42

Tab. VII shows the main reasons for rejections in 1981, namely pharmaceutical-chemical documentation unsatisfactory, bioavailability data unsatisfactory, clinical documentation unsatisfactory, clinical documentation unsatisfactory plus other reasons, no benefits proven, side-effects, price, azo-dyes, other reasons.

G. Kristinsdottir

Table VIII. 202 registration applications handled in 1981.

The use of	Number of applications	Approved	Rejected	Same conclusion as in Norway	Sweden
External assessors	5	4	1		
Evaluation reports from Norway and/or Sweden	50	28	22	31	36
External assessors and evaluation reports from Norway and/or Sweden	8	7	1	4	6
Inter-nordic projects	5	2	3	2	3
Total	68	41	27	37	45

Tab. VIII shows how often external assessors were used, how frequently evaluation reports from Norway and/or Sweden were used in the assessment, how often the Norwegian and/or Swedish reports were used in combination with external assessors report and how many applications were handled in inter-nordic cooperation. The numbers of approved applications and rejected are shown and to which extent we reached the same conclusions as Norway and Sweden.

Table IX. Number of registered specialities
1.1.1978-1982

Year	Drugs	Forms and strengths
1978	708	1133
1979	730	1160
1980	728	1164
1981	746	1189
1982	798	1278

Tab. IX shows the number of registered drugs and different forms the last 5 years.

Table X.   Registered specialities 1.1.1982

	Number of drugs	Number of forms and strengths
Foreign	687	1132
Domestic	38	56
Veterinary drugs (all foreign)	73	90
Total	798	1278

Tab. X shows the breakdown of the number of registered specialities the 1st of January 1982 into foreign, domestic and veterinary products. In addition I would like to explain that there are also on the Icelandic market some 400 generic drugs produced according to monographs in pharmacopoeias and other formulas.

Table XI.   Applications for limited import of unregistered drugs

Year	Number of applications
1978	571
1979	492
1980	588
1981	658

Tab. XI shows the number of applications for limited import of unregistered drugs during the last 4 years.

I have outlined for you the drug registration procedure in Iceland. The registration is published in a Speciality Register which is published annually as said before and in between updated by quarterly addenda. Following registration it is the duty of the State Drug Inspectorate to control that the conditions for registration are met. This includes the control of advertisement and the price.

I would like to conclude, that although there are obvious constraints in operating an adequate drug regulatory mechanism in countries with such small populations as Iceland, it can still be done satisfactorily provided that the bulk of applications remains on a reasonable level. It is obviously also of greatest value to have access to scientific evaluation reports from other sources as a basis for a national decision.

EXPERIENCE IN THE GRAND DUCHY OF LUXEMBOURG

L. Robert

Chairman of the EEC Committee for Proprietary Medicinal Products, Luxembourg

With your permission, Mr. Chairman, I would like, first of all, and more particularly for our colleagues coming from countries far away from Europe, to say a few words concerning the Grand-Duchy of Luxembourg, situated between France at the south — the Federal Republic of Germany at the east — and Belgian at the west and north border.

The total population is about 360 000 inhabitants in an area of 2600 square kilometers. In order to illustrate this even better that means something like 100 km from north to south and 50 km from east to west, at its largest surface.

Luxembourg is an independant nation since the Treaty of London in 1839 and even if it is considered as an industrialized country there is no chemical and no pharmaceutical industry. For the supply of medicaments, the population therefore depends entirely on importation.

Luxembourg has no University, no research centre and the hospitals are, of course, in relation to the size of a country of 360 000 people. This situation makes the undertaking of toxicopharmacological and clinical trials practically impossible.

In order to demonstrate the contribution such a small country can offer to illustrate the subject of our discussions, one must consider the general situation at the end of 1945.

Like most European countries, Luxembourg had been partly destroyed and a high percentage of the population having been in deportation, the sanitary conditions were rather precarious. So one of the major tasks of the Government, at that time, was to ensure the supply of essential medicaments. This was not an easy task because the situation in the surrounding countries was equally bad. This state of things continued until 1948 to 1950.

Then the economic climate changed rapidly. The industrial rise was spectacular and the need for medicaments, as a consequence of the deficient state of health of our population being considerable, created, in addition to the well known pharmaceutical firms, an increased number of more or less important new companies.

This evolution was, of course, favoured by the fact that in those days, in most countries, there was no specific legislation concerning this economic sector.

As a consequence of this situation the production of pharmaceuticals also increased very rapidly, pharmaceuticals more or less well studied and even very often commercialized without having been submitted to any quality control.

I will give you only one example. At the end of 1950 one could find on the market of some of our countries a whole set of proprietary medicinal products having been exposed to ultra violet rays.

The active substances of these medicaments were well known compounds and they were marketed as Dia-aspirin - Dia-phenacetin and even Dia-penicillin - Dia-streptomycin.

The manufacturing procedure was the following:

U.V. lamp	active substance	excipient
	(e.g. aspirin)	

One may imagine now that the so irradiated active substance was incorporated into the excipient in order to produce tablets of 500 mg aspirin and pretend then that this treatment had increased the therapeutic activity of this aspirin.

But this was not the case.

The manufacturer assured that the U.V. rays had transferred the therapeutic activity of the aspirin into the excipient and he prepared his Dia-aspirin only with the excipient. The same procedure was followed for the preparation of Dia-penicillin and Dia-streptomycin.

Neither, at that time, did we dispose of any legal possibility allowing the Government to prohibit the marketing of these products which were not only evident frauds but, even more serious, represented a real danger for ill people.

But the most astonishing fact was that these so-called medicaments were prescribed by doctors and reimbursed by our social security system.

I could multiply these examples but this would lead us too far from our present discussion.

The general situation was that, most of the time the authorities were not informed of the marketing of medicaments containing new active principles, knew nothing about their therapeutic properties and any potential danger for the consumer. For these reasons the legal provisions, the authorities had to take, were always several years behind reality. So, it was impossible to keep an up-to-date list of medicaments which could be dispensed on medical prescription only.

The situation was unacceptable and the Government had to take action.

It was very clear that before legislative measures could be set up in this field it was absolutely necessary to know all about the proprietary medicinal products actually on the market and it was therefore essential to create a system of obligatory registration of medicaments before commercialisation.

This task was very difficult to realise at that time because the European countries, from which we imported our pharmaceutical products, except France, did not dispose of specific legislation and a small country like ours could not adopt the French arrangements.

Inspite of these difficulties a draft bill was elaborated and presented to Parliament in 1954.

Unfortunately, the mentality at the time was not prepared to accept such innovations. The opposition of all concerned parties - doctors - pharmacists - industry - was very strong. So it took 4 years to overcome all obstacles and only in May 1958 the bill was finally published and came into force.

The major topics in this text were:

— Definition of the expression " proprietary medicinal product."

— The obligation for all proprietary medicinal products to be covered by an authorization delivered by the Minister of Public Health before their commercialisation.

In order to receive this authorization the person responsible for the marketing of the product had to make an application giving the following information:

1. Name of the medicament.

2. Name and address of the manufacturer.

3. Name and adress of the applicant.

4. Complete composition of the product.

5. Therapeutic indications.

6. Pharmaceutical forms and packaging sizes.

7. Wholesale price — proposed public price and public price in the exporting country.

8. Indications concerning eventual advertising to the public.

To this information the applicant had to add:

— a complete analytical dossier;

— a document established by the authorities of the exporting country certifying that the medicament was legally on their market, in conformity with the indicated composition.

In requiring from the applicant the analytical data, and we must not forget that we are in 1958, one could, at least, expect that the manufacturer, disposing of these analytical methods, would check the raw materials and the finished product. As could be expected often the responsible managers of pharmaceutical companies, and not only of small ones, protested against these measures, arguing that working as conscientiously as they did, there was no reason to check the finished product.

In asking the authorities of exporting country to assume a certain responsibility concerning the exported medicaments one could expect that these medicaments were at least of the same quality as those destinated for domestic consumption.

This was really a minimum requirement.

CONCESSIONNAIRE.		FABRICANT.
Composition.		Champ d'application.
		Groupe thérapeutique.
Formes thérapeutiques.	Prix.	Mode de vente.
		Publicité.
		Divers.

At the same time we proceeded to the classification of all registered proprietary medicinal products into 16 major therapeutic groups — each group comprising a certain number of subdivisions.

MINISTERE DE LA SANTE PUBLIQUE
Service de Contrôle des Médicaments
Demande d'immatriculation

Nom du produit:

Nom et adresse du laboratoire d'origine:

Nom et adresse du représentant ou du concessionnaire:

Indications thérapeutiques majeures:

Formes thérapeutiques mises sur le marché:

Conditionnements:	Prix grossiste	Prix pharmacien	Prix public	Prix public pays d'origine

Est-ce que le produit fait l'objet d'une publicité extra-professionnelle?   non

Dans l'affirmative, veuillez donner les renseignements y relatif.

N.B.   Toute modification de quelque nature que ce soit affectant un des renseignements figurant sur ce document doit être notifiée immédiatement à l'Inspection des pharmacies, Service de contrôle des médicaments, 3, rue Auguste Lumière, Luxembourg (Tél. 438.11)

With all this information a kind of simplified data-sheet, in 2 copies, was drawn up.

Formule qualitative et quantitative complète

(Renseignements strictement confidentiels)

Méthodes d'analyse. (ces renseignements doivent être consignés sur une feuille séparée, annexée au présent document)

Certificat de conformité

Nous certifions par la présente que la composition de la spécialité pharmaceutique faisant l'objet du présent document a été contrôlée et qu'elle a été trouvée conforme à la formule déclarée ci-dessus.

L'autorisation prévue à l'article 2

de l'arrêté royal du 6 juin 1960

a été accordée sous le n° 172 5 21 F 6

One of the copies was classified in alphabetical order according to the patent name of the products, which makes it possible to dispose, without delay, of the most important indications concerning each proprietary medicinal product.

The second copy was filed according to the therapeutic groups. So, one could find out all registered specialities containing a given active substance, for instance all medicaments containing penicillin or barbiturates or digitoxin and so on.

When the work was finished a catalogue was published in the official journal, indicating the names of all the proprietary medicinal products admitted for sale — their pharmaceutical forms and packaging sizes — the conditions for delivery, that is to say delivery outside pharmacies, in pharmacies, sold over the counter or under medical prescription — narcotics, and finally an indication concerning the reimbursement of the product by the national health service.

Beside the fact that from this time on the governmental authorities were able to keep the pharmaceutical market under control, they succeeded also to make a first clean up of the situation. As a matter of fact, by the end of the 1950's the number of proprietary medicinal products in circulation had been evaluated, by checking in pharmacies and through wholesalers, at something like 16 000 to 20 000 units.

In 1961 this number had been reduced to more or less 5600 patent names, which represented 7500 to 8000 pharmaceutical forms.

This was not a negligible result but of course all these medicaments did not yet correspond to the quality — safety and efficacy requirements in the modern sense. But this is true today in all our countries; the problem of " old " products.

Let us now see what kind of measures had to be brought into play in order to reach these results.

First, on the material side.

— The printing, the forms and the data-sheet.

— Rooms for the storage of the registration dossiers.

— Two files, one for the alphabetic classification and one for the filing according to the therapeutic groups.

Secondly the man power requirement.

All the work was done, in two and a half years, as I said, by two persons — one pharmacist and one typist.

To keep updated this registration system, that is to say the inscription of new products or the suppression of older ones, is a relatively easy task.

CONCLUSIONS

I have tried to explain, as briefly as possible, the method undertaken, at a difficult time, by a small country, whose human — material and scientific resources are very limited, in order to get under control an economic sector as vital and as complex as the pharmaceutical sector.

To-day the situation has greatly improved. Practically all countries producing pharmaceuticals, as we heard this morning, dispose of specific legislation assuring the quality, the safety and the efficacy of the manufactured medicaments.

For Luxembourg the situation has also changed greatly since our country entered into larger communities like Benelux and the EEC.

Inspite of these facts it is indispensable for a country depending entirely for its supply of medicaments on importation, to foresee a certain number of safety measures.

I see these measures on 3 levels.

— First it is absolutely necessary to set up an obligatory registration system for proprietary medicinal products before commercialisation. This is a " conditio sine qua non."

— Secondly, in order to guarantee the quality of the medicaments the application for registration has to be accompanied by a document, established by the authorities of the exporting country, certifying that the manufacturer is legally authorised to produce medicaments and that his plant is regulary controlled by these authorities.

— Thirdly, in order to guarantee the conformity of the exported batches to the declared composition, they must be covered, either by the control report signed by a qualified person or by a document like the WHO certificate.

SITUATION IN LUXEMBOURG NOW

J. Loutsch-Weydert

Chef de la Division de la Pharmacie et du Médicaments, Luxembourg

Taking over from Mr. Robert, I have to stress two points

1. We are a country of 350000 inhabitants only, without pharmaceutical industries implanted, without any university.

It follows that we are the last ones to be opposed in any way to a free circulation of drugs between countries with harmonized legislations, for the very simple reason that we cannot afford opposition. We are utterly dependent on neighbours for drug supply. Our greatest concern is sufficient security for our population.

2. Before the introduction of European directives, of which you have heard a great deal already, or in any case are familiar with, importation of drugs was rather more difficult. The difference or absence of legal measures in the exporting countries made it difficult for us to apply always the same standards in our examination of drugs when registering them. You have heard already that registration was introduced in 1958 in our country and completed by 1963.

The introduction of EEC directives, meant a simplification for us.

To put it in a nutshell: we do hold the admittedly bold view that a drug that has been registered by EEC agreed standards since the date of application (20 nov. 1976), which means that it had been screened by scientists of one of our EEC fellow-countries and found good enough for their nation, cannot hold sudden and evil surprises for our own population just by having crossed the border into our country.

It follows that we have the same registration as our fellow member-states, the same application form, the same procedure, mapped out in EEC-Directives, the same marketing authorization, but that the process tends from our side towards mutual recognition. It is not yet automatically granted.

Every application is examined by a board of experts appointed by the Minister of Health to prepare the decision for him. But we do have a quicker procedure in the event of an existing authorization granted recently (after implementation of EEC Directives) by an EEC member state.

One great difficulty of this system of ours lies in the presence of so-called " old " products in our neighbour countries, meaning those present on the national markets before 20 nov. 1976 i.e. implementation of EEC Directives, and not in need of an EEC-conform application until 1990. For these there is a temporary hold-up to free circulation.

It remains to be said that traditionaly there were good contacts with partners of the Benelux countries (Belgium and Netherlands) contributing in creating a temporary common Board of Registration called " Service Commun d'Enregistrement Benelux " for the 3 member states. This experience, though thoroughly satisfying from a scientific point of view, proves in the end quite expensive for the insufficient results and has to be brought to a close probably at the end of this year. Amongst other reasons partly unknown there are, sadly, linguistical reasons, in this case difficulties of translation. We keep of course cordial and close relations with these partners, as well as with our immediate neighbours, France and Germany, with whom we have no linguistical problem whatsoever, which extremely simplifies direct administrative relationship. The very important question of a common language cannot be over emphasized when approaching matters of this kind. Translation is not the answer to every problem.

When mutual recognition is impossible, as in the case of a new substance, we have experts in France and Germany, as in Belgium and the Netherlands, who take over the scientific evaluation of the application. But mostly we prefer an application for a product already registered in our neighbour states.

Analytical controls are currently made by samples in our country. As you can judge by what I have tried to tell you, Luxembourg tries to work in a truly European spirit of cooperation.

We think, as the smallest partner of the European Community, that this is the key to our security in drug supply.

SWISS DRUG REGULATORY AUTHORITY

P. Fisher

Director of the Intercantonal Office for the Control of Medicines, Switzerland

INTRODUCTION

An International Scheme for the Evaluation of Drugs (SED) was discussed at the WHO Regional Committee for Europe Meeting that took place in East Berlin from the 14-19 September 1981. The background to the scheme was set out in a WHO Regional Office for Europe Report ICP/DPM 003 (S) Rev. 1, dated 6th August 1981, headed Consultation on an International Scheme for Drug Evaluation.

During the East Berlin meeting a number of representatives of WHO Euro Member States declared their opposition to this scheme and the final resolution agreed at this meeting was that further consultation should take place with interested bodies and Member States so that a revised scheme could be re-submitted to the next Regional Committee for Europe Meeting which is due to take place in Copenhagen from 26 September-2 October 1982.

One of the declared objects of the Second ICDRA Meeting in Rome is " to examine models for effective regulatory operation in countries having limited resources." It is therefore relevant both to consider the proposals set out in the WHO Euro SED scheme and to outline what is already available to meet developing countries' needs in this connection.

SED Scheme

The WHO Euro document explained that the scheme is designed " to assist the many WHO Member States who do not have adequate facilities for the regulatory evaluation of new drugs." However, during the discussion that took place at the East Berlin meeting it became clear that developing countries are much more concerned with existing drugs than with new drugs. Indeed, developing countries, largely as a result of WHO initiatives, are now primarily concerned with those drugs included in the WHO Essential Drug List.

During the East Berlin meeting several representatives of Member States in the Regional Committee mentioned that they had grave reservations on the feasibility of the proposed scheme and whether indeed there was a real need for such a scheme. Amongst the points raised by delegates were the following: confidentiality of data, creation of an additional and supranational registration body, absence of a legal framework and absence of a system of rights of appeal. In addition there was the important issue about who would take the financial responsibility in cases where product liability was in question.

Another key issue raised in the discussion at East Berlin was that the SED Scheme would need substantial funding and that unless industry was willing to help (which was doubtful), the cost would fall on developing countries themselves.

Needs of Developing Countries

This subject was discussed at some length at a recent WHO meeting on the subject of " Basic Elements of Drug Legislation and Drug Regulatory Control for Developing Countries " (DAP/81.3). This meeting was held under the chairmanship of Mr. Yeap Boon Chye, Director of Pharmaceutical Services, Pharmaceutical Division, Ministry of Health, Kuala Lumpur, and included a large representation from developing countries themselves. The consultation dealt with all aspects of drug regulatory control in developing countries, including imports, manufacture, drug registration, quality control, information and clinical trials. One of the main conclusions of this meeting was the developing countries' chief concern with problems connected with quality and information of established drugs imported into their countries. The report states that " most developing countries may not initially afford to build up an extensive quality control or assessment system. Effective use of the WHO Certification Scheme is therefore recommended for quality assurance of imported drugs."

WHO Certification Scheme

This scheme has been in existence since 1975, but is still insufficiently used by WHO Member Countries. The purpose of the scheme is to provide assurance on the quality of exported pharmaceutical products moving in international commerce. Importing countries need to be reminded that product certificates are issued by the competent authorities of the exporting country at the request of the importing authorities. These certificates relate to individual products. It is worth emphasizing that a competent authority in the importing country can request from the competent authority that issued the product certificate, further technical information relating to the product. This could include, for instance, a request for approved information data, e.g. indications, contra-indications, precautions, side-effects, etc. (It is obviously necessary for developing countries to employ competent staff to handle the information provided under the WHO Certification Scheme). Switzerland, in common with many other developed countries, has provided training in registration procedures and quality control to personnel from many developing countries.

In addition the international pharmaceutical industry, including specifically, the Swiss pharmaceutical industry, has provided many training posts in quality control to government employees from developing countries.

Other Information Data Available from WHO

At the previously mentioned WHO Consultation Meeting on Basic Elements of Drug Legislation and Drug Regulatory Control for Developing Countries (DAP 81.3) it was stated that "Information on conditions of approval for registration in the country of origin of a drug will be helpful for decision making. Developed countries may also have a contribution to make in fostering and, on request, participating in technical cooperation programmes."

Although the main focus of interest by developing countries is on established drugs, it is agreed that they also have a need for information both on new drugs and on new indications and contra-indications of existing drugs. This need, however, is already being met by WHO's Drug Information Bulletin, which is issued on a quarterly basis. This bulletin includes information and notifications from Regulatory Authorities in Member States on newly registered products and major changes in, or withdrawals of, product authorizations. In addition, WHO issues, from time to time, information on special pharmaceutical products addressed to all drug regulatory authorities.

As can be seen, therefore, the needs of developing countries for information on drugs and regulatory matters are already being met though it is worth emphasizing that sufficient use is probably not being made of existing schemes such as the WHO Certification Scheme and the WHO Drug Information Bulletin.

An example of the way the WHO Certification Scheme is not being used to the best advantage is the fact that the intercantonal office for the control of drugs (IKS), the competent authority in Switzerland, received approximately 4,500 requests for product certificates in the last 12 months, but only 5% of these requests were accompanied by enquiries for additional information on such matters as indications, contra-indications, etc.

Mutual Recognition

It is considered that many of the problems connected with drug regulatory matters, including those involving developing countries, can be met by adopting the principle of mutual recognition. As an example, a Scheme for the Mutual Recognition of evaluation reports of pharmaceutical products (PER) has been initiated by the European Free Trade Association

(EFTA) and is primarily intended to avoid duplication of the individual procedure by the different national authorities.

Another example of the value of such mutual recognition schemes is the operation of the Pharmaceutical Inspection Convention (PIC). Under this convention, authorities from member states are enabled to accept inspections made by corresponding authorities in other participating states. It is thus no longer necessary to send officials between participating states for the inspection of manufacturing facilities when the drugs concerned are manufactured in one country and imported into another. The cooperating countries involved in this PIC scheme include, in addition to the 7 EFTA countries, a further 7 countries, and it is worth emphasizing that the number of countries cooperating in this scheme has steadily increased over the 10 years since it was first established.

CONCLUSION

Apart from the other problems connected with the proposed SED scheme, it would inevitably be seen as a supra-national registration body, providing yet one more regulatory barrier with different rules from other regulatory agencies. It would inevitably combine the more onerous features of each nation's existing systems and would delay even further the process of innovation. In this connection it is worth emphasizing that developing countries have as great a need for new drugs, for instance to combat tropical diseases, as developed countries.

We commend the concept of these international conferences of Drug Regulatory Authorities as a forum for the discussion of common problems and experiences of national drug regulatory authorities from both developed and developing countries. In our view, we believe that serious consideration should be given to holding such meetings on an annual rather than a biennial basis. However, it is strongly recommended that time should be allocated at the next ICDRA meeting for a progress report to be made on the conclusions and recommendations of the preceding meeting which would include, inter alia, the points raised in this paper.

REGULATORY CONTROL
OF IMPORTED DRUGS

THE QUALITY OF IMPORTED MEDICINES

B. Huyghe

*Inspecteur Général, Inspection Général de la Pharmacie,
Ministère de la Santé Publique, Belgium*

INTRODUCTION

The interference of public health authorities in the field of medicines has no other purpose but to guarantee the " good quality " of drugs and, at the same time, the marketing of them at a reasonable price and in sufficient quantities.

However, the concept of " quality " has evolved over the years. At present it goes far beyond the mere identification of the product or the variety of the plant as described in the pharmacopoeia, even beyond the chemical conformity between the contents of, say, a tablet and the notified formula: " quality " is now expected to cover a set of elements and criteria which medicinal drugs should meet to be labelled " good " quality products.

Among these elements and criteria are:

— *the pharmaceutical qualities*, such as the quality of the active ingredients and of the excipients, the physical qualities of the preparations, their homogeneity, their microbial contamination, their bioavailability, the content conformity, the intended delayed, slow or sustained release, and the stability under various storage conditions;

— *the safety of the medicinal preparation* when used normally;

— *the efficacy* in the proposed indications.

All these elements together add up to the concept of quality of a medicinal product with the present state of our knowledge and of the development of the medical and pharmaceutical sciences.

The primary goal of the public health authorities must be to guarantee such quality. Yet this is only possible through an array of legal, regulatory and administrative requirements, licensing procedures and controls, covering the whole lifespan of the medical product. This process starts even before a medicament is put on the market — during the clinical trials —, continues through the controlled phase and extends beyond the consumption by the patient, passing along the various stages of registration, manufacture, distribution, storage, delivery and information supplied to the medical and pharmaceutical professions and to the public.

This procedure is fairly simple in the case of drugs manufactured in the country. However, delicate problems arise in relation to " *imported* " products.

Possible doubts as to the quality of imported medicines

For obvious reasons, there is normally no way for public health authorities to carry out whatever controls in the exporting countries on the manufacture of medicines and they can never be confident of the ways in which the quality control and the evaluation of the toxicological, pharmacological and clinical data have been performed. Consequently, a number of unknown points remain with respect to the medicinal product e.g.:

— *the person responsible* for manufacture and quality control: his academic record, his qualifications, his responsibility inside the company, his human and moral qualities;

— *manufacture*: industrial facilities, laboratory, equipment, working conditions, technical aspects and hygienic conditions, the implementation of the G.M.P.'s;

— *quality control*: bathwise testing of all the components, control during manufacture and on the finished product, or sampling procedures, the standards applied, the strictness of the evaluation, the security measures envisaged and applied to rule out possible errors;

— *the toxicological and pharmacological trials*, the prescribed norms and protocols, their implementation, the circumstances in which these tests on animals are run, their critical and statistical evaluation;

— *the clinical trials*: the prescribed standards and protocols, the authorization prior to any clinical tests, the techniques used (therapeutic impressions or more modern, objective and critical methods such as double-blind studies), the critical and statistical evaluation of the results, the careful observation of possible side effects, interactions, contraindications, etc.;

— *the registration of medicinal products*: authorization prior to marketing, criteria applied during evaluation, authority in charge of evaluation (approved experts or government commission); in the latter case, its composition, its terms of office, the systems used, the risk-benefit ratio accepted, strictness and earnestness of the investigation.

All these elements cast more or less serious doubts to which the public health authorities of the importing countries should find a solution, which should suffice to avoid the marketing of medicines of doubtful quality or of ' quack ' products, but which, at the same time, takes account of the technological, scientific and economic capabilities of the importing country.

Elements affecting the measures taken by the importing countries

It is beyond doubt that when preparing measures intended to guarantee the quality of medicines, account should be taken of a range of elements which directly or indirectly limit the importance of these measures and direct them in one way or another.

These elements include:

— The economic situation. Developing countries, for example, have far less financial scope than developed nations. The same applies to other areas where the means to be implemented are highly dependent on the overall situation in the country. The scientific infrastructure is such a case; the administrative services should have qualified staff to carry out this quality control. Apart from being qualified, this staff should also be conscious of its responsibilities and duties towards society.

— The medical pharmaceutical infrastructure of a country should also be considered. Indeed, it would seem difficult, for instance, to allow on the market very effective medicines with a very specific activity — and hence difficult to handle — without competent personnel able to make a precise diagnosis, to correctly administer the medicines and to take adequate action if necessary.

— The choice of medical products is also strongly influenced by the social security scheme or mutual benefit societies. In view of the present economic situation it is quite unthinkable that a compulsory social security scheme should reimburse any medicine at any price. Therefore, priorities should be established and a judicious choice should be made. Of course, this will not fail to affect, either directly or indirectly, both the measures to be taken when issuing a marketing licence and the controls.

Apart from these elements affecting the measures to be taken with a view to guaranteeing the quality of imported medicines, there are some others with depend on the geographical and political situation of the importing country. Among these are:

— the impact of the climate on the stability of the product in hot and damp countries, which may not be beneficial to adequate storage of the product;

— the existence of regional political entities which various countries have joined to form a larger whole with the aim of finding solutions to their common problems, e.g. BENELUX, the EEC, the Council of Europe, EFTA, the Nordic Council. The establishment of common guidelines aiming at similar control systems may largely influence the measures taken to ensure the good quality of medicines imported from a member country;

— local health problems may also bear upon the choice of the measures to be taken. Diseases related to climate or to other environmental factors may exemplify this point;

— finally, due to insufficient financial means, it will be necessary under certain circumstances to have regard to the most pressing needs of the majority of the population rather than to try and find a solution to all the problems, however large, facing a minority group.

All these factors must be considered when choosing the measures that should be taken to try and find a solution to the doubts that still remain with respect to imported medicinal products.

In the light of these facts, our work today is to examine the regulatory control of imported drugs.

THE EXPECTATIONS OF DEVELOPING COUNTRIES

DRUG REGULATORY PROCEDURES
THE EXPECTATIONS OF DEVELOPING COUNTRIES

A.C. Zanini

National Secretary of Health Surveillance, Ministério da Saúde, Brazil

About two years ago, I attended the Annapolis Conference. At that time, I had been responsible for the Brazilian Drug Control Agency for only one week. I was convinced that I knew how to solve the problems of the Agency. Now, after two years, I am not so sure that I know how to solve them. Therefore, I am very interested in attending this Second International Conference of Drug Regulatory Authorities because the meeting raises many issues which are very important in improving drug control in Brazil.

I should like to start which a few problems I had to tackle on my own work over the past two years and some solutions I have tried to find for solving them. By sharing my experience with you, I hope to be of some help to other representatives of developing countries having similar problems.

In all countries, people want the best drugs, i.e. the best natural and synthetic pharmaceutical products and the best herbal remedies. But it is still an open question what is " best " for each country. In some countries, the availability of only a few hundred products on the market is considered to be the best solution, while other countries consider that 30,000 or more products on the market are necessary for adequate medical care. Other issues are the freedom of prescription by physicians, the need for " orphan " drugs advocated by scientists and the different views expressed by politicians in parliamentary debates. As far as the developing countries are concerned, I would submit that the following needs should be taken into account by the drug regulatory agencies:

(1) developing countries need drugs suitable to meet their special needs in the control of prevalent parasitic and other infectious diseases;

(ii) the modern pharmaceutical industry is heavily engaged in research of new drugs for the cure of the aged; however, this is not a high priority in developing countries where the average life-span of the population is much shorter than in North America and Europe;

(iii) the appropriate use of existing drugs, currently available, offers greater benefits to the patients than " new " drugs which are not well known to the physicians and are more expensive. For instance, the new antihypertensive drugs are not only more expensive but their use requires greater skills and involves more risks than the well known and widely used antihypertensives;

(iv) because of the high prices of modern over-the-counter drugs, these products are replaced in developing countries by herbal remedies, pseudo-homeopathic drugs and other " native " natural products. All these drugs have not been tested for safety and efficacy like the modern drugs, but their empirical use is related to local traditions and customs. It is, however, important to evaluate their safety and efficacy and to identify the ingredients they contain; this may also lead to the development of new requirements for their regulatory control;

(v) the list of essential drugs proposed by WHO has been, in a few countries, a starting point for ensuring the availability of the most necessary drugs; for many developing countries, the WHO list represents also an approach to the reduction of medical exsspenses through a limited number of pharmaceutical products currently available on the market.

I am a physician and a pharmacologist and for the past six years I have been actively involved in working on essential drugs, i.e. no more than 300 active substances and 600 products. Since I took my present position in the Drug Control Agency, I had to deal with 4,000 substances and more than 30,000 products on the Brazilian market, including many fixed combinations, produced by more than 400 manufacturers. In this market situation there are obvious problems facing the Drug Control Agency. The solution of these problems is not easy and the necessary measures could not be implemented suddenly.

Our main objective has been to know which products were on the market-place in Brazil and which substances they contained, since it became evident that without such knowledge the Agency could not fulfill its responsibilities in drug control. A computerised system was used for the processing of information on more than 30,000 products on the market and the first print-out was produced just a few weeks ago. I was surprised to find out that, because of the use of different names for the same substances, more than 12,000 active substances had been listed by the computer. After a first review of the names listed, the number of active ingredients was reduced to about 4,000 substances and many " natural " ingredients.

Another important issue is related to the influence of unfair control of drug prices. The more the prices of essential drugs are reduced, the more the opposition of the pharmaceutical industry grows. If a wrong policy on price control is implemented, these essential drugs tend to disappear from the market after some time, whereas secondary products continue to be marketed.

As already mentioned, the Drug Control Agency has had the financial and computer resources adequate to identify the pharmaceutical products available on the Brazilian market. However, the main problem to be solved now is to find ways and means to ensure that only those products that are safe, effective and properly labelled remain on the market.

I hope that this brief presentation on some special problems of drug regulation in Brazil may help other developing countries in focusing their efforts and in setting their own priorities. I find that the discussions at this Conference are very useful and I hope that most representatives of other developing countries will share this view.

THE EXPECTATIONS OF DEVELOPING COUNTRIES IN THE CONTEXT OF DRUG REGULATORY CONTROL

M.P. Sihombing

Director For Drug Control, F.D.A. Indonesia
Ministry of Health R.I., Indonesia

I would like to express my deep appreciation to the organizing committee for the invitation to attend this conference and to be given the opportunitiy to present my views on the expectations of developing countries in the context of Drug Regulatory Control.

Since the first ICDRA in Annapolis, 28-31 October 1980, some useful information such as information from U.S. FDA have been continuously disseminated. It is hoped that other recommendations decided in the first conference will be realized, so that developing countries can take more benefit from this international collaboration.

Drug registration in developing countries

With the ever increasing number of drugs marketed in the developing countries, control of marketed drugs is urgently needed to ensure that only safe and efficacious drugs are available to the people. Today, registration is required in most developing countries before drugs are marketed and efforts have been made to evaluate their safety, efficacy and quality. But some constraints are faced in the implementation of drug registration, mainly lack of manpower resources, experiences and inadequate organized registration units. Experts from several disciplines needed to assess the technical data are usually not sufficient, while the available experts need more experience to undertake evaluation and assessment.

Even though some developing countries have initiated systematic review of the currently marketed drugs, results of comprehensive reviews of old drugs, such as DESI — programme undertaken by FDA, would be very helpful.

Claims and contents of labelling and advertisements approved in the country of origin are sometimes different from the ones submitted in the developing countries.   In this context, sufficient information on approved drugs is very useful for developing countries.

In some cases, new drug applications are submitted in developing countries which are not yet approved in the country of origin.   Some of them with data on clinical trials which are not, or not yet, conducted in the country of origin.   In this regard information on approval or disapproval of investigational new drug applications and justification for the decisions are useful for the developing countries.

Drug circulars and drug information provided by WHO are useful, particularly in re-evaluation of marketed drugs.   Since drug monitoring systems in developing countries do not exist, or are still in an early stage, it is hoped that the role of WHO as a focal point for the collection and transmission of information should be intensified.

Quality Assurance in developing countries

Good Practices in the Manufacturing and Quality Control of Drugs as recommended by WHO has been generally adopted in the developing countries, but it has not been fully implemented.

Quality control by the Government cannot be undertaken properly mainly due to inadequate capability of quality control laboratories as well as insufficient qualified drug inspectors.

Although some developing countries have encouraged the production of finished products locally, almost all raw materials are still imported.

It was noted that some suppliers of pharmaceutical raw material who do not have production and quality control facilities, relabel raw materials from other sources for exportation.   In this case quality of the product is doubtful.

Considering the above mentioned reasons, adequate measures are necessary to safeguard the developing countries against the importation of substandard raw materials.   The certification scheme of WHO needs to be strengthened.

Some developed countries, like USA, restrict the importation of raw materials only to companies approved by FDA.   Information about the approved products and producers would be very useful for developing countries in addition to the certification scheme of WHO.

Expectation of Developing Countries

In view of the constraints faced by developing countries, it is expected that international collaboration be aimed at the following objectives:

— Strengthening of drug legislation appropriate for developing countries;

— Strengthening of the execution and quality of drug evaluation and registration;

— Improving the capabilities in quality assurance of marketed drugs;

— Safeguarding developing countries against the importation of sub-standard drugs, including raw materials.

Possible collaborative activities relevant to the achievement of the above mentioned objectives are the following:

— Exchange of information;

— Training, seminars, exchange of experts and experience.

Exchange of Information

Information exchange was much discussed during the first ICDRA. With reference to those discussions, information expected by developing countries is identified as follows:

1. Regulations, guidelines and standards. These will help the developing countries in understanding the legal basis of the decisions made by the respective countries and could also be used as references for the development or improvement of drug legislation, guidelines and standards in developing countries.

2. List of approved drugs which could facilitate the developing countries in knowing the status of certain drugs in other countries.

3. Basic data such as U.S. FDA's Summary Basis for Approval that could also function as reference to improve the quality of decisions made by developing countries. In this respect, we really appreciate that FDA, U.S. has sent us regularly the Summary Basis for approval as one of the positive outcomes of the first Conference. We do hope that other countries can do the same.

4. Approval and disapproval of applications for investigational new drugs (IND) and their justification.

5. Disapproval of applications for new drugs (NDA) and its justification.

6. Change of status of marketed drugs because of suspicion of safety risks or ineffectiveness, and new restrictions to guarantee safety, including requirements for labelling or new restrictions on marketing status.

7. Results of review of old drugs, such as DESI programme, undertaken by U.S. FDA.

8. Products and producers of raw materials approved by FDA for importation to the respective country.

9. Information by request about analytical methods. For this purpose a list of reliable laboratories is needed.

Depending on the confidentiality, sensitivity and bulkiness of the information, beside the role of WHO, exchange of information can be carried out on direct and continuous bases, or upon request.

Training, Seminars, Exchange of Experience

Efforts have been made by WHO to help the developing countries in improving their capabilities in the formulation and implementation of national drug policies and management through consultancy schemes and training.

Among ASEAN countries, technical cooperation in pharmaceuticals has been started in collaboration with WHO. But the efforts have been hampered due to limited financial resources.

To improve the capabilities of Drug Regulatory Control Authorities, training of personnel, exchange of experts and experience is needed. It will be useful for developing countries to know the list of training programmes and institutions appropriate for training available in the developed countries. It would also be helpful if the Food and Drug Authorities in the respective countries could arrange training programmes.

Exchange of experts and experience could be made by providing experts from developed countries to visit developing countries and the opportunity for the Drug Regulatory Control personnel to visit relevant institutions in developed countries.

The above mentioned arrangements cover the following aspects:

— Drug evaluation and registration;

— Monitoring of drug adverse reaction;

— Experimental pharmacology and clinical pharmacology;

— Drug inspection;

— Quality control laboratory;

Drug supply and utilization audit.

It is hoped that developing countries will be informed and given the opportunity to participate in any seminars related to drug registration and quality assurance organized in developed countries.

Prominent problems and constraints faced by developing countries with regard to drug regulatory control, particularly in the field of drug registration and quality assurance, have been presented.

Expectations of developing countries through International Collaboration have also been briefly formulated.

It is hoped that this Conference will elaborate realistic and feasible collaborative programmes and plans of action. Most important are the follow-up and implementation of the agreed activities.

DRUG REGULATION IN AFRICAN COUNTRIES NEEDS AND EXPECTATIONS OF THE EIGHTIES

E.C. Chidomere

Food and Drugs Administration, Federal Ministry of Health, Nigeria

1. Manpower or trained personnel

In my opinion, the greatest need of African countries in the area of pharmaceutical development and drug control, is the training of the necessary personnel. Manpower is very much important because it is people, human beings, NOT machines, that have to work with the equipment and technical facilities in the laboratory; people will draft the Drug legislations and regulations; and execute their provisions, and people will formulate and execute National Drug Policies. The trained professionals and personnel will be the first available to achieve all this. It is also the qualified personnel that can benefit from any relevant additional training aid programmes.

In West Africa, for example, in Gambia and Sierraleone, there are only about 3 and 10 registered pharmacists respectively. In Sierraleone, only 2 or 3 of the 10 are in the civil service. In Tanzania (East Africa) there are only about 80 registered pharmacists (1980).

There is no doubt that pharmacists are a very important professional group whose training brings them into direct contact with pharmacy and drug laws, and the manufacture and quality control of drug products. How can we then achieve significant pharmaceutical development and effective drug control in all its ramifications, in a country with only 3 or 10 or 50 qualified pharmacists for the entire population. The acute shortage of trained personnel also affects other relevant professional and scientific disciplines, such as: medical doctors, clinical pharmacologists, toxicologists, microbiologists, chemists, biochemists, technologists.

2. Technical facilities

There is the need to establish Universities and allied institutions in many African countries, or alternatively to establish them on a regional or geographical basis to serve a group of deserving countries. Such institutions will not only train the necessary manpower, but also can serve as referral or resource centres, providing essential technological and scientific expert services to the Government Drug Control Authority. This arrangement is working well in some African countries, such as: Egypt, Sudan, Zimbabwe, Kenya, Tanzania and Uganda.

Two years ago the International Federation of Pharmaceutical Manufacturers Associations (IFPMA) had offered, through the World Health Organisation, to set up a pilot scheme for quality control training. Places would be made available to 25 suitably qualified candidates from government-controlled laboratories in third world countries to receive QC training at the industry's expense in industry laboratories. So far, 10 candidates have come forward and, to the spokesman's knowledge, two have completed their training, both in Britain.

There should be more international support to African countries to establish their Drug Quality Control Laboratories. Such support may be in terms of monetary aid, supply of necessary equipment and the training of necessary personnel. Such training should be mostly undertaken in the countries concerned, and should be tailor-made to suit the local conditions.

3. Drug Control Legislations

There is no doubt that developing countries need to have, or make adequate and effective, drug control legislation and regulations in the present situation of world-wide proliferation of drug products, when " drug dumping " has become a common feature in the technologically disadvantaged nations. Developing countries that do not expect to have all the necessary trained manpower and technical facilities (for laboratory quality control) in the immediate future, must make and rely upon adequate and effective drug control legislation and regulations for the registration and importation of drug products.

This is especially important for those developing countries that depend heavily upon imported drug products. Some African countries import one hundred percent of the drugs consumed. An effective safeguard, therefore, is to place the onus of responsibility on the exporter or manufacturer for the quality of his products. This is especially important when it is realized that the Drug Regulatory Authorities of many exporting countries do not exercise any legal controls over drug products made in their territories for the overseas export market. African countries can therefore achieve this through legislation by means of enacting such requirements that would offer assurance of the quality and acceptability of the drugs they receive.

It is my opinion that the requirement for: " Certificate of Registration in the Country of Origin " and " in any other countries " (non-specified), is NOT enough. In addition a requirement for: " Certificate of Registration and Sale in at least one major developed country " such as U.K., U.S.A., Canada, Europe, should be a *sine qua non* condition for African countries. It is in fact a *sine qua non* condition for some industrialized countries like Portugal. Also, the Federal Republic of Germany, Netherlands and Turkey make similar requirements.

Finally, there is the need for many African countries to update their existing drug legislation or even make new ones so as to make adequate provisions for necessary regulations for effective control of drugs. There is also an important need to establish the necessary administrative machinery for the Organization of Drug Control, depending upon the model that suits each individual country. In this latter need, help will be needed by many African countries.

4. National Drug Policies on Drug Importation and Utilization

There is no doubt that it will be easier to control fewer drug products in a country where their flow and use are controlled. This can be achieved by deliberate National Drug Policies that:-

(*a*) Limit importation of certain categories of drugs in order to encourage their local manufacturing;

(*b*) Limit utilization by implementing an Essential Drugs List or using National Formularies.

Formulation of National Drug Policies on drug importation and utilization are especially important for African countries that depend very heavily on imported drug products. In a free enterprise economy, no amount of legislation may prove effective in controlling the number of imported drug products unless there is a Drug Policy limiting drug importation and use. It has worked very well for the few African countries that have implemented National Drug Policies.

The following African countries limit their drug utilization by implementing Essential Drugs Lists, or by adopting National Formularies. For example:-

Egypt	— (i) Egyptian Pharmacopoeia (E.P.) (ii) Egyptian Hospital Pharmacopoeia (E.H.P.)
Zimbabwe	— PEDLIZ (1981) (Proposed Essential Drugs List for Zimbabwe)
Ghana	— Ghana National Formulary
Tanzania	— Tanzania National Formulary.
Uganda	— Uganda National Formulary.
Sudan	— Sudan National Formulary (1979)
Togo	— Essential Drugs List (reducing the number of imported drugs from 3,500 to 1,200) (1980).
Upper - Volta	— National List of Specialities.
Zambia	— Zambia National Formulary.
Kenya	— Limited Essential Drugs List, for use in Government Hospitals only.

There is no doubt therefore, that a National Drug Policy limiting drug importation and use, is an essential strategy for achieving effective drug control. Besides, such a policy leads to a more rapid pharmaceutical development. Efforts should be made by those African countries that have none, e.g. Nigeria, to formulate National Drug Policies which will suit their needs and economic conditions.

5. What Developing Countries Expect from The Developed Countries

The present situation, in which many developed and drug exporting countries do not make legal provisions for the registration of drugs made for the overseas export market, is certainly bad enough, and should be looked into by concerned international organizations such as the ICDRA. With the present exception of the U.S.A., many other industrialized nations do not exercise any legal controls over drug products made for the overseas export market. Some, such as the Federal Republic of Germany and Switzerland may make voluntary registration, while the U.K. provides only for the registration of biological products, e.g. sera, vaccines, blood and blood products.

It is my opinion that the current international pharmaceutical development aid programmes are not enough, especially for the African countries. There should be less talk and more action. From available data, it would appear that most of the initiatives are being left to the over-stretched World Health Organization. I think that individual Governments and Multinational Drug Companies who make huge sums of profit, should be more involved in giving support to African countries. Individual multinational drug companies should plough back some of their profit in the development of pharmaceutical education, training of local manpower in universities and other institutions, and the supply of necessary equipment and technical facilities to establish local quality control laboratories.

Although the current international pharmaceutical aid programmes need to be stepped up, it is quite encouraging to know that worldwide pharmaceutical industry is now more willing to help the developing countries, than was previously envisaged. Also the industry is becoming more sensitive to the complaints about unethical marketing practices in the developing countries. For example, at the recent Congress of the International Pharmaceutical Federation (F.I.P.) held in Vienna, Austria (September 1981), Mr. S.M. Peretz, executive vice president of the I.F.P.M.A. announced the adoption by the IFPMA council, of a Code of Pharmaceutical Marketing Practices, for its members. Among other provisions of the Code, the industry undertook " to provide scientific information with objectivity and good taste, with scrupulous regard for truth, and with clear statements with respect to indications, contra-indications, tolerance and toxicity ".

6. Co-operation Among The Developing Countries

The last, but certainly a very important need in this series, is that African countries must help themselves. The initiatives to improve existing conditions or to get external aid must come from the African countries themselves.

There is no doubt that there is this need for co-operative arrangements among the African countries in the area of pharmaceutical development and drug control.

Available data indicate that there is a better co-operation among the other Third World developing countries of the S.E. Asia, Latin America and the Caribbean, in the area of pharmaceutical development and drug control. However, one must not fail to mention the co-operation among the Arab North African countries, and also among the Franco-phone West African countries. For example, the Heads of the Drugs Regulatory Authorities of the French-Speaking W. African countries, together with those of Tunisia and Morocco, met in Libreville, Gabon, in December 1979, to examine the problems of quality control of drugs in their countries. And the Anglo-phone W. African countries have taken the first step towards co-operation, through the establishment of the West African Pharmaceutical Federation, an agency of the West African Health Community — which is an inter-governmental organisation.

Finally, there is no doubt that African countries need to evolve better co-operative and collaborative arrangements, at present generally lacking, among themselves. This co-operation will be best achieved on a regional or sub-regional basis, as the case may be. There is need for co-operation in the areas of: manpower training, harmonisation of drug legislation, registration of drugs, laboratory quality control, drug inspection, advertising and labelling of drugs, information exchange, national drug policies and management, establishment of essential drug lists and national formularies, and joint ventures in drug quality control, monitoring and information exchange, drug Production and Procurement (for the smaller Countries).

CONCLUSION

Perhaps the most important of what remains to be said is to re-emphasize that African countries themselves must take the initiative to get things done. This initiative is working well for the other third world countries that have recognised the importance of working together in regional or sub-regional groups, in order to solve their various Pharmaceutical Problems.

ZIMBABWE SITUATION

D. Galletis

Registrar if Drugs, Drug Control Council, Zimbabwe

Looking around at the various invited countries and organizations, I think I am correct in saying that Zimbabwe is probably the youngest nation represented at this conference. We have only last week celebrated our second birthday. From what I am about to say, I am certain that you will think of my country, not as an undeveloped country, but the best of the Third World under-developed countries.

I wonder how many representatives — apart from those of you from Africa itself — will even have heard of Zimbabwe. Perhaps I can be given a little time to establish just where it is. Zimbabwe is surrounded by other countries: South Africa to the south, Botswana to the west, Zambia to the north and Mozambique on the eastern border. There are Savannah Lands and Mopani Forests on the west side, these are surmounted by the Victoria Falls on the Zambezi River in the top left hand corner. The northern border separates us from our Zambian neighbours by the Great Zambezi River on which the Kariba Dam is built. The southern border divides us from South Africa by the Limpopo River, and there is a range of mountains (Inyanga - the Chimanimani) in the east. The main areas of civilisation are situated along a central spine running from south-west to north-east. Bulawayo is in the bottom left: Salisbury, the Capital in the upper right. The urban aspect of Zimbabwe is highly developed in the major towns and cities.

Area	390 590 Sq Km (150 804 Sq Miles)
Population	7.700.000 (77% of the populations is Shona)
Capital	Salisbury, Population 670 000
Religion	Traditional, Christian
Language	English, Shona, Ndebele
Economy	Industries: minerals (gold, asbestos, nickel, copper, coal and chromite) food processing, textiles Export crops: Tobacco, Cotton, Sugar Domestic Consumption: Corn, Livestock, Millet

The fight against drug abuse is essentially a matter for the closest international co-operation. I presume this is the administrative system by which States aim to help prevent the diversion of drugs from licit supply to illicit use. If therefore there is any help or advice we can give from our experiences we should of course be very glad to give it. Circumstances and problems differ in most countries and I hope that my Council and I can be of assistance. From the reports I have received there is certainly no real drug abuse problem in Zimbabwe. We are not concerned today with the controls on narcotics and non-medicinal poisons.

Control varies in degree according to the hazard associated with the substance. At present there are *three* classes of substances.

Dangerous Drugs (Narcotics) Act

Are of course those which are capable of producing addiction. Although these narcotics are the responsibility of the Ministry of Health, the staff at Drugs Control Council actually do all the work.

Hazardous Substances and Articles Act

There are no medicinal substances or mixtures of substances which may endanger the health of human beings, or domestic or wild animals, etc. by reason of its toxic, corrosive, irritant, inflammable action. Excluding *any* " drug " to which provision is made in the D.D. Act or in D & A.S.C. Act, they are mostly household, agricultural, industrial and horticultural poisons. This Act is administered by the H.S. board.

Drugs and Allied Substances Control Act

Medicinal substances which can only be sold in registered premises — pharmacies, general dealers etc.

The term " drug " in our legislation to me, is erroneous; it should be changed to " medicines ".

As far as I am aware the Drugs and Allied Substances Control Act contains extracts from the South African Medicines and Related Substances Act 1969 and the U.K. Medicines Act 1968. I like to think we have taken the best from both these acts for our own situation. The act provides for the evaluation of the quality, efficacy and safety of drugs, control by licensing of their manufacture, marketing and promotion, export, import and distribution, and for breaches to be punishable as criminal offences. The registration procedure started with all " new " drugs that were marketed after the 1st October 1971. This allowed for " old " drugs to be continued to be sold providing they were on the Rhodesian market prior to that date. As from the 1st August 1981 all drugs on the market were " specified " and applications for their registration were required to be submitted to my Council by the 1st January 1982.

The same criteria were established for veterinary drugs. The first date was 1st October 1978 and the date for this class for all " old " drugs was the 1st April of this year 1982.

A Manufacturer's Licence is granted when certain standards in good manufacturing practice are seen to be in operation. Inspections are carried out locally by pharmaceutical inspectors (due to lack of suitable staff this is not as often as I would like) with respect to premises, equipment, storage facilities, quality of ingredients, qualifications of persons working with drugs, arrangements for safe keeping, production methods etc.

I understand that in the U.K. similar standards are enforced in the issue of wholesale dealers licenses for use where drugs are distributed but not manufactured on the premises.

A Registration Certificate is required by all pharmaceutical companies in order that a medicinal product may be marketed in Zimbabwe. This certificate is granted following assessment by my council's Experts Committees, as to the quality, efficacy and safety of the product in question. Stringent guidelines are laid down on the pharmacological, toxicological and clinical data required by the Committee before recommending that the product be registered. During the evaluation of the preparation, indication for use, any contra indications, precautions and warnings thought to be necessary, are brought to the attention of the Committee. Information given to the medical profession, together with any advertising, must be in accordance with Council's recommendations.

A Certificate of Free Sale in the country of origin is a necessary requirement for obvious reasons. This is sometimes not practical, e.g. anti-malarial drugs are seldom sold, if ever, in Europe.

A screening procedure has recently been implemented prior to the evaluation of a drug to be considered as urgent for the Zimbabwe market. There are TWO criteria, of which at least one must be met, these are:

1. The product is a significant therapeutic advance over already available drugs.

2. Availability of the drug represents a significant financial saving to the public.

To meet these criteria applicants must submit with their drug applications a case of not more than 500 words on why the Drugs Control Council should begin to evaluate the application.

Measures to control the method of sale are also contained in the Acts and Regulations. A product is placed in certain categories, N., PP., PR., P., H.R. or HRA. etc. The first two may only be obtained and sold in pharmacies on the production of a prescription issued by a medical practioner, dental surgeon or veterinarian.

We also have a special category for amphetamine type of drugs with special unique restrictions, details of which I will elaborate, if necessary. Similar restrictions also exist for other drugs, which we call specially restricted drugs, these are mainly the psychotropic substances. I think

I am correct in saying that we are unique in our control of these two types of drugs.

Regulations list the substances which are to be available only on prescription, specify exemption in terms of maximum strength, quantity etc. and the general prohibition on the sale.

The act defines advertising and sale. There are advertising prohibitions on drugs used for the treatment of certain listed serious conditions, each category for distribution has advertising conditions related to it.

The general rule being that no advertising may be false or misleading or likely to deceive, say, other persons about its character, value, quality, composition, merit or safety. No person shall for example advertise any drug which contains codeine or its salts, amphetamine type drugs and specially restricted drugs — to members of the public.

In the context of medicinal products there are also, or may be, drugs of abuse. Both the Drugs and Allied Substances Control Act and the Dangerous Drugs Act should complement each other — in my view they should be consolidated into one Act.

In controlling medical products, a nation may find itself on the horns of dilemma; it always runs the risk of doing too much or too little.

To do too little is not to be exacting enough: is to allow recourse to medicines presenting established or potential risks which exceed the known or probable benefits: is obviously failing to perform its allotted task, which is to provide the community with the best possible protection against such a risk.

But one can also do too much. There is an anxiety to achieve maximum safety at any price which can lead to require producers of medicinal preparations to provide an ever-increasing abundance of documentation, evidence from more and more onerous tests, and thus an ever lengthening time lag to occur between application for registration and the marketing of the product. The result is that research of new medicines is slowed down. This delay can affect the health of a nation just as much or more than some unsuspected side effects.

It is therefore necessary to strike a balance among the systems enforced in some western countries; one must find a method whereby its success is in keeping within the bounds of bureaucracy, delays and other constraints which restrict the search for new medicines. A small country like ours must make use of all information received from the western sophisticated countries without becoming bureaucratic and endeavouring to maintain the middle of the pendulum path.

It is very easy for us, with the small staff and financial resources for carrying out inspections, to accept information, albeit in good faith, that may not meet the standards set for quality and efficacy, let alone the safety of drugs.

What is the answer? I ask, and I hope we are here this week to obtain the answer.

In the context of the subject matter for this Conference they are only a few points which I feel are very relevant.

The documentation that is required by Regulatory Authorities is very extensive, whether they are for the major western nations, or small

Regulatory Authorities, like ourselves. When the evaluation is done, I wonder how much of this is necessary? And how much is duplication? As other major western countries have also made their own assessments and findings on the same product, if we could surely have some universally acceptable standard which would be acceptable to all nations without each country being a mere rubber stamp, I think this will not only help the smaller agencies but also help the industry. I feel that autonomy is necessary because conditions do vary from country to country. I think there is a need to standardise the pharmacological classification of drugs and certain labelling requirements.

In my opinion the category for distribution and shelf-life (in particular) can be determined by the regulatory authority. We must agree that the stability of a product will vary because of climatic conditions in various countries.

Documentation data to be provided must be similar in most countries. Most western nations do have the resources of both staff and, of course, the finances to be able to carry out sophisticated experiments and clinical trials, as well as performing tests on both animals and humans. All records and batch data relating to a particular batch, including raw material analytical reports, during manufacturing up to the final product and authorization for the release, including the inspections of factories, is easily accessible to the western nations. We in Zimbabwe, do not have this for products manufactured in our country, but it is readily and easily available for products manufactured outside our borders, and thus we have to rely very heavily on the batch data that is supplied by the manufacturer.

Without pointing any finger at anybody we all know that this information can be falsified. I would, therefore, like to have an assurance from the authorities of an exporting country, backed by WHO, that the batch data supplied and the good manufacturing practice is carried out to the standards that would normally be acceptable to all of us.

May I indulge and keep you for just a few more minutes. Generic prescribing, I would say, would be an important aspect that developing countries would encounter, mainly from a financial aspect. This is really a function of my Council, but I would recommend that the cost of many drugs could be reduced by having a standard package and label for Third World Countries. The size of the generic name could be increased and the trade name reduced. An attempt to formulate a common policy, to minimise packaging costs and have special packs for developing countries.

We would like a more rapid notification of decisions made by other regulatory authorities on both new and old drugs. Particularly when registration is refused and the reason for such refusal is significant. Some nations do not sometime or other either withdraw registration or place west nations on the percentage of ingredients or even certain label warning requirements. This is also of great importance to my Council.

My Council would like some advice on a universally acceptable simple definition of a galenical — homoepathic medicine, and for a herbal remedy. Why and how these products are not registrable in your countries.

Despite these few pitfalls, some not very serious, we have, in my opinion, a country such as ours, achieved more than one would ever hope for. Drugs control started in 1971 and for the first ten years of the life of my Council, we have been almost isolated from the rest of the world. The size of our staff has been very small and it is my personal opinion that the Council and its small staff should be congratulated on its magnificent work.

We have a fairly sophisticated computor programme, which I can explain if you so wish after the meeting, second to none on the African continent. I am certain that we should, and can, and will, all work together to try to formulate some practical solution to all our problems.

May I, in concluding, leave a point or two which occurred to us in thinking of likely problems. Legislate for your own requirements and situation, the simpler the system, the easier it is to control. Perhaps one of our main tasks, in this Conference, is to consider how far the elements of control can be created separately from an effective general system of control of medicines.

I like to think of Zimbabwe, with its present legislation and control, as the most developed of the under-developed countries.

DRUG REGULATORY AUTHORITIES - AFRICAN REGION

F.S. Boi-Doku

Who Regional Office, Africa

INTRODUCTION

1. Of all the problem confronting developing countries in the field of the provision of health care, none is more difficult than the formulation of a drug-policy, which would ensure the uninterrupted availability to their population of essential drugs of established quality at a cost that the people can afford. The pace of development of drug regulatory mechanism is slow in the African Region of WHO because the difficulties and constraints are many; and the issues on which policy decisions are called for are complex and require the deepest consideration, as their implications and effects could be both serious and extensive. For, we are talking here about a policy area which involves legislative enactments to regulate the importation, storage, supply, destribution, quality control, labelling, information, advertising and of course export, manufacture and proper utilization of drugs. Exportation and production of drugs are not prominent issues in our countries at present, but nevertheless require considerable attention even now. Policy formulation and implementation in all these areas require certain pre-requisites, the lack of which constitutes contraints on development. Some of these are:

(i) Lack of trained manpower of all categories for policy formulation, sector planning, management and implementation etc.;

(ii) Lack of financial resources arising from low per capita G.N.P. which means lack of resources to procure drugs in quantities adequate for the needs of the populations, especially those in the rural areas;

(iii) Lack of local production of drugs has many causes but the end result is over-dependence on imported drugs;

(iv) Lack of drug quality control facilities in African countries means over dependence on overseas manufacturers for the quality of drugs procured.

2. An ad hoc committee appointed by the WHO Regional Director for Africa in 1978 to look at the whole area of drug policy and management, identified the shortage of drugs as the most pressing problem facing health services in the Region. Of course, African countries have made strenuous efforts at disease prevention and health promotion, and the beneficial effects of these will be realized in due course. However, as of now, the lack of drugs to cure simple illnesses such as malaria, pneumonia, diarrhoea, which are claiming thousands of lives every day, makes the populations lose faith in the health services and undermines their best efforts to mobilize the population in the fight against disease. We must, therefore, have an adequate supply of effective drugs, whatever else we do, and especially in the area of Primary Health Care. For, drugs are essential not only to save bodies but to win minds and souls to the cause of better life. So, our Plan of Action on drugs for the period 1982 to 1985 has the following broad objective: " To promote the development and establishment in each country of National Drug Policy (NDP) in support of National Health Programmes, particularly, Primary Health Care ". It also has the following sub-objectives: " To promote:

1. the establishment of lists of Essential Drugs;

2. the establishment of procurement and tender procedures;

3. the improvement of drug distribution within countries;

4. local drug formulation;

5. quality control of drugs and vaccines and

6. adequate drug information.

The various activities which will be undertaken in full collaboration with the countries within the scope of these objectives will, we hope, eventually ensure the uninterrupted availability to our populations of effective, safe essential drugs of established quantity at a cost that the people can efford.

Ensuring quality, safety and efficacy of drugs

3. In this area WHO collaborates with Member States to upgrade existing quality control laboratories. It does this by providing Short-Term Consultant (STC), when requested, to identify problems, propose solutions and evaluate activities. The aim is to establish or strengthen 10 national quality control laboratories by 1990.

4. WHO also helps to train local staff in simple techniques; it also trains professionals and promotes advanced training of postgraduates in quality control, production methodology and technology and in research. It does this by the award of fellowships of which 26 have been made between 1978 and 1981 to benefit 16 countries. Provision has been made

to award more fellowships in quality control of drugs and vaccines during 1982.

5. Meetings have been organized at sub-regional and regional levels so that Chief Executives could meet and exchange ideas and receive information on activities in the Region. One such meeting was held in Beira in 1981 and a meeting of Chief Pharmacists is currently taking place in Salisbury, Zimbabwe. Literature on drug policies, quality control etc. is made available to Member States.

6. WHO Member States are urged to use the WHO certification scheme and, in fact, many of them have become members of the scheme, thus enjoying all the protections prescribed. In addition to this, AFRO has adopted a " List of Essential Drugs " for a " Group Bulk Purchase " scheme, in which WHO guarantees the quality, at source, of drugs procured.

7. Without any wish to bore you, I will ask you to examine the six sub-objectives of our plan.

You will find that they, and the various activities planned, are calculated to eliminate ultimately the constraints, which I have mentioned at the beginning of this paper; namely: (1) lack of trained manpower; (ii) lack of financial resources; (iii) lack of local production of drugs (iv) lack of quality control facilities and last (v) lack of effective distributive systems within countries.

Expectations of Importing Countries

8. It seems reasonable that importing countries should expect manufacturing countries to export only drugs of proven efficacy and quality, which are of the same standard as those used in the exporting countries. To ensure this a scheme exists whereby WHO is informed whenever a drug is banned in any country and this information is then disseminated to Member States. Also literature accompanying drug packages should be the same throughout the World and translations into local languages meet with the approval of the local health authorities.

9. Since climatic and other physical conditions in developing countries differ from those in manufacturing countries, these factors should be taken into consideration during formulation and packaging of drugs for export.

10. In order to prolong shelf life and obviate harsh conditions of transportation within developing countries, only the freshest batches of drugs should be exported.

11. Pricing structures for drugs for export to developing countries should be examined with a view to offering preferential treatment especially for drugs intended for use at primary health (PHC) level. WHO is trying to do this by the proposed Group Bulk Purchasing scheme, which involves pooling orders together.

12. Unethical advertising should be discouraged. Here individual countries should protect themselves by having an officer or committee to review drug advertising and related matters.

THE ROLE OF INTERNATIONAL
AND REGIONAL ORGANIZATIONS

THE ROLE OF THE EEC IN ENSURING ADEQUATE STANDARDS FOR DRUGS IN INTERNATIONAL COMMERCE

N. Bel

Head of Pharmaceutical Division, Commission of the European Communities, Belgium

INTRODUCTION

International cooperation is a great asset in the field of public health. This is certainly the case where standards on quality, safety and efficacy of drugs are involved. The Commission of the European Communities therefore warmly welcomes the organization of this conference of regulatory authorities on a worldwide scale. The EEC especially thanks the organizers of the conference for their invitation to participate.

The role of various international organizations in the field of drugs can be quite different as can their influence and authority outside their geographical area of activity. These differences largely depend on the extent of their competences (ratione materiae or ratione loci), the objectives they are pursuing and the legal instruments which they have at their disposal to implement their policies.

The EEC now comprises 10 Member States. Together it represents 30% of world production of drugs and half of world's drug exports. It has created an important body of high level standards in drug registration. Indeed, the EEC is a supranational body when contrasted with international organizations of the classical type which have been created to institutionalize intergovernmental cooperation. I shall first of all explain this difference and then deal with specific aspects of public health in which the EEC is involved and the way responsibilities for public health are shared inside the EEC. The bulk of my paper will, however, focus on the activities of the EEC in adopting common standards for quality, safety and efficacy of drugs. I will close by explaining the significance of common rules for drug registration inside the Community and the effects of these rules outside the Community.

The Role of the EEC in Comparison with International Organizations of The Classical Type

There is a considerable amount of international cooperation in the field of public health. First of all, there are the different organizations in the framework of the United Nations, amongst which WHO takes a predominant place. Outside this framework, various ways, of international collaboration have been instituted by international treaties. Limiting ourselves to Western Europe, there are e.g. the Council of Europe, the Nordic Council, the Benelux, EFTA, the OECD and finally the European Economic Community, which I have the honour to represent here today. In order to avoid overlapping of activities, an adequate level of collaboration has been reached in recent years between the EEC, the Council of Europe and WHO, and especially its Regional Office for Europe.

The main difference between EEC and other forms of international collaboration in Western Europe is the supranational character of the EEC. The EEC represents international cooperation of a very specific nature. The Rome Treaty has provided the EEC with its own Institutions endowed with legislative power, e.g. the Commission and the Council of Ministers. Moreover, the European Commission acts as executive of the Community with the explicit task of supervising the implementation of Community law. Finally the Community has its own Court of Justice which interprets the Community rules.

No matter to what international treaty dealing with drug legislation Member States might adhere, they still have to comply with the Rome Treaty and with Community rules established by its institutions. In addition subsequent legislation in Member States will lose its validity if it is contrary to Community legislation.

This Community legislative power is exercised by the European Commission and the Council of Ministers. This legislation of a federal character is however implemented and enforced by the authorities of the Member States. I will come back to this point later on.

How Competences in public health issues are divided between the EEC and Its Member States

The competences of international organizations in public health affairs are either of a general nature or limited to specific issues. The EEC belongs to the latter category. The EEC as an economic organization has not an overall competence in public health matters. The overall competence for public health is expressly left to the Member States. This results clearly from Article 36 of the Treaty. However, the Community has very specific competences where national health measures interfere with the establishment and functioning of the common market.

A common market presupposes primarily free circulation of goods, services, persons and capital and fair competition. It is unnecessary to explain in detail why national requirements for drug registration might constitute major barriers to international trade. It is therefore in this very field that the EEC has been very active in promoting common standards. It has done this by harmonizing pharmaceutical legislation with the help of the legal instruments the Rome Treaty has put at its disposal, namely the binding directive.

Since its creation in 1958, the Community has gone a long way and enjoyed much success in harmonizing legislation or drug quality, drug safety and drug efficacy. The initiative of the Commission has thus provoked a real codification of drug standards applicable in all its 10 Member States. In doing so the Community has actually translated into legislation that which was up till then only the subject matter of discussion in professional, scientific or governmental circles and which was (at most) considered merely desirable criteria or to be recommended in most parts of the world.

However banal the legal requirements for drug registration might seem to be now, manufacturers have to be reminded occasionally to fulfil these minimum legal obligations before being authorized to put their products on the market.

The Community requirements not only give a solid basis for authorizing products but also a legal basis for withdrawing them from the market when they no longer conform to the requirements.

In carrying out the task of suppressing obstacles to trade through harmonization of pharmaceutical legislation of the Member States, the European Community has assumed a highly difficult but positive task.

Harmonization activity in the Community is always dominated by concern for public health. This principle is expressly laid down in the preamble to our EEC directives, and I shall quote directive 65/65/EEC:

" Whereas the primary purpose of any rules concerning the production and distribution of proprietary medicinal products must be to safeguard public health, (...) "

A further guarantee that the protection of public health constitutes the leading principle of harmonization of drug registration in the EEC is the fact that the proposals of the Commission can only be adopted by unanimous vote of the Council of Ministers, in which all the Member States are represented.

Thus, the concern of each Member State for the protection of the life and health of its citizens is integrated in the Community rules. These Community rules for drug registration are a combination of scientific, professional and governmental experience in the field.

Before transmitting its proposals to the Council, the Commission consults governmental experts, representatives of science, industry and consumers. The Council, before discussing the proposals of the Commission, consults the European Parliament and the Economic and Social Committee of the Communities. Adoption by the Council is prepared by its own group of government experts. In that way, 5 Council directives have been adopted which now cover the registration of drugs in the whole Community.

Let us now see what are the concrete contents of these Community rules for drug registration.

Community Rules on Quality, Safety and Efficacy of Drugs

What nowadays seems to be banal and a minimum standard for assessing the quality, safety and efficacy of drugs was still a controversial point at the moment of the adoption of the first pharmaceutical directive in 1965.

This directive subjected the marketing of drugs in all Member States to authorization to be delivered by the health authorities. The introduction of a marketing authorization is the cardinal point of all Community legislation in this field. Indeed, the effect of this authorization system is that any drug on the market without such an authorization is illegal and the persons concerned liable to prosecution. If any drug is not, or is not anymore, in conformity with the conditions under which it was authorized, the marketing authorization has to be withdrawn. If a finished product is not in conformity with the quality standards laid down in the authorization, the product has to be withdrawn from the market.

The second main feature of Community pharmaceutical legislation is the fact that the process of manufacturing is subject to a specific manufacturing license. The guarantee of quality in drugs marketed in the Community exists therefore on 3 levels:

1. adequate design of the drug prototype,

2. adequate manufacturing and batch controls,

3. adequate and detailed documentation and information concerning the product.

The guarantee of the characteristics of a drug has to be furnished by the person who applies for a marketing authorization. He has to demonstrate that his product is of good quality, safety and efficacy. If not, the marketing of his product will be refused. Or, in the terms of Article 5 of the first pharmaceutical directive, "The authorization ... shall be refused if after verification of the particulars and documents ... it proves that the proprietary medicinal product is harmful in the normal conditions of use, or that its therapeutic efficacy is lacking or is insufficiently substantiated by the applicant, or that its qualitative or quantitative composition is not as declared ". The directive gives very precise indications on the means by which the applicant has to prove the quality, safety and efficacy of his product and what kind of data he has to present to the health authorities.

Essential for the proof of quality, safety and efficacy are the results of the analytical, toxicopharmacological and clinical trials.

First of all one must comply with the European Pharmacopoeia, or failing that, the national Pharmacopoeia of the Member States. There is at present a wide consensus on analytical quality criteria in the Community even if, here and there, we still discuss the specificities of certain methods of determination or certain details for stability testing.

The drafting of the data to prove the *safety* of the drug has created more problems. The standards were finally formulated in a flexible way to allow an application which could take into account the progress of the state of art. The Directive on Standards and Protocols dealing with the toxicity data indicates in broad terms what the toxicological and pharmacological tests in animals must show. First of all the potential toxicity of the drug and any dangerous or undesirable toxic effects that may occur under the proposed conditions of use. Secondly the tests have to show the pharmacological properties of the product, in both qualitative and quantitative relationship to the proposed use in human beings.

The directive gives also a brief description of what kind of data the applicant has to procure under the following headings: single dose toxicity, repeated dose toxicity, foetal toxicity, reproductive function, carcinogenicity, pharmacodynamics and pharmacokinetics.

It appeared to be even more difficult to elaborate workable criteria for the performance of clinical test to demonstrate *efficacy*. No exact legal criteria could be formulated which would be appropriate to assess the optimal balance between efficacy and toxicity.

The essence of the criteria for clinical trials formulated in the directive is that they should be carried out in the form of " controlled clinical trials ". Where the effect of the product cannot be objectively measured, the double-blind method of controlled study should be used. Statistical methods are to be used where such is necessary to determine the therapeutic effect. An extensive chapter is devoted to the presentation of particulars and documents regarding clinical trials. The kind of conclusions the investigator has to draw from the experimental evidence is of course essential.

All these criteria for the performance of the different tests were elaborated and adopted in 1975. Subsequently there appeared to be no need to modify the criteria substantially. The only updating which has appeared to be necessary consists of adding to the existing criteria the submission of data about bioavailability and mutagenicity. Experience with the application of the directive has taught that however extensive experiments on animals and clinical trials may be, drug safety cannot be significantly increased. There seems to be no longer any relation between costs and benefit. Hence, other ways and means have to be sought to increase drug safety.

An effective way is a more intensive assessing and evaluation effects on a sufficiently high number of patients during the marketing of the product. The European Community is active in this field also. I will come back to it later on.

The next important question is by what means the Community legislation guarantees that the product effectively manufactured conforms to the concept of the product and the conditions of the marketing authorization. To this end the obligation for the manufacturer to have a manufacturing license has been introduced in directive 75/319/EEC.

The presence of a pharmacist, or of otherwise scientifically qualified persons, has been imposed to survey the production process. He has to take the responsibility for ensuring compliance with the control methods approved by the health authorities. The scientific qualifications of these persons has been laid down in detail in the second pharmaceutical directive itself. Such a person has to certify that the manufacturing and the controls have been performed for each batch in conformity with the marketing authorization. Moreover, he has to keep precise records of his activities. This will enable the health authorities to carry out their inspection tasks.

With the extensive concentration in the European pharmaceutical industry of the last 20 years, equipment has been completely renewed. As a result, manufacturing standards are now very high in the EEC. Regular national inspections are obligatory under Directive 75/319/EEC. WHO, or more detailed GMP rules, are applied in all Member States.

National Application of Community Legislation

As has already been said previously, the responsibility of the EEC in in public health is limited to those questions that directly interfere with the establishment of a common market. The introduction of Community criteria for drug registration has taken place through implementation of the directives into the national medicines acts. This means therefore that the Community criteria are actually applied by the national health authorities of the Member States in granting national marketing authorizations. The decentralized application of a federal legislation entails sometimes differences in individual decisions. Consequently, the question arises how these differences in application can be limited to a minimum in a common market. To this end different ways are open. Firstly, the Commission of the European Communities has to survey the application of Community law. Secondly, the Court of Justice of the Community has the last word in the interpretation of the Treaty and of Community law deriving from it. In case of infringements of Community law, the interested parties can request the Court to give an opinion.

A specific instrument of coordination for applying common criteria on individual drugs is the Committee for Proprietary Medicinal Products. This Committee is composed of the heads of the pharmaceutical departments of each Member State. This Community institution has been created especially to give opinions about the quality, safety and efficacy of specific drugs when there are divergences between the authorities of the different Member States. In addition the CPMP has developed an important activity in the field of drug monitoring since its creation in 1975. In its bi-monthly meetings the Committee examines series of drugs which are raising problems with regard to side-effects, warnings to be given, indications to be limited, etc. Thus the CPMP plays an important role in establishing a common approach to drug registration policy in concrete cases.

The ultimate objective of harmonization in the EEC is to bring about a situation similar to the one which exists on a national market. Member States have increasingly to accept that the authorities of other Member States examine the merits of a product on their behalf.

Doubts were raised if such a recognition of the decisions of foreign authorities would be justified on the basis of the general criteria fixed by the directives. In this context it was decided to draft documents elaborating in more detail the criteria of the directive on Standards and Protocols, to give more guidance on how to interpret the requirements. To this end two working groups of the CPMP have been charged with this difficult task, one for safety, the other for efficacy, presided over respectively by Dr Griffin of the United Kingdom and Dr Dukes of the Netherlands. The activity of these working groups has resulted in the elaboration of 6 documents on the performance of different toxicological tests and a number of documents about the performance of clinical trials concerning different therapeutic groups.

The leading principle in elaborating these guidelines is flexibility in order not to impede the experimenter in his research for new drugs which society obviously needs. These documents will have the form of recommendations.

With 5 directives, a set of guidelines and a permanent coordination committee, the Commission of the EEC thought it justified to propose to Member States the mutual recognition of each other's marketing authorizations. Indeed, the Commission is of the opinion that there are now sufficient guarantees for Member States importing drugs from other Member States regarding quality, safety and efficacy. Moreover, these guarantees are substantiated in a complete documentation about all the merits and aspects of the drug concerned.

The Implications of Community Legislation for Extra-Community Trade

In proposing mutual recognition, the Commission of the European Communities has expressed the conviction that drugs authorized, manufactured and labelled in conformity with the requirements of the directives fully meet modern standards of public health for all Member States.

In the same way, countries outside the EEC can benefit from similar guarantees when importing medicaments produced and marketed in Europe in accordance with EEC directives.

In my opinion, their major concern about protection of public health is covered by three main aspects of these directives: premarketing testing, quality of manufacture, proper evaluation by governmental organizations.

1) The premarketing testing of the drug has been performed inside the EEC in accordance with scientific criteria which are internationally recognized. This means that the basic analytical testing, including stability tests, all toxicological and pharmacological studies in animals and most of the clinical trials need not to be repeated in the importing country.

It became evident, during our first meeting in Annapolis, that a formal harmonization of these testing criteria was a very difficult, and perhaps impossible, task. Nevertheless, the Commission of the European Communities considers that tests which adequately prove the quality, safety and efficacy of a drug should be considered equivalent in other parts of the world. They should not be repeated simply because there may be slight variations in testing requirements between different countries. Such unnecessary repetition not only constitutes an important waste of resources which could otherwise be devoted to innovative research, but it is also a major ethical problem because human and animal testing is at stake and should be reduced to a minimum.

2) All products manufactured inside the EEC are submitted to regular official inspections whereby international GMP rules are applied. As most of these products are also put on the EEC market, they also have to conform to the specifications laid down in the European Pharmacopoeia and in the approved documentation submitted for the marketing authorization. Again these specifications are properly checked by official inspections and samples which are analysed by official laboratories. In each firm, a highly qualified person is responsible for the quality of each batch. Records of the analysis of each batch can be obtained by the interested governmental bodies.

3) The drug has been properly evaluated by highly competent governmental agencies before a marketing authorization is issued. This authorization can always be withdrawn when the benefit-risk ratio appears to be no longer favourable. The marketing authorization also lays down the conditions of marketing which may in addition appear on the labelling and the package leaflet, or in the information to doctors.
In my opinion these documents could, if requested, also be presented by manufacturers to the health authorities of countries outside the Community. The documents could provide adequate guarantees for third countries taking into account their responsibility for public health when importing drugs from the Community.

4) A supplementary contribution of the EEC to the promotion of quality, safety and efficacy of drugs in international trade will be found in two important new documents, namely the so-called product summary and th evaluation report. The introduction of these documents can be expectede in the near future. The product summary will contain all relevant information about the product and will be annexed to the marketing authorization. The evaluation report will substantiate the reasons why the health authorities consider a product as safe, efficacious and of good quality. The evaluation report will be an important element in the system of mutual recognition of marketing authorizations granted by other Member States. However, there is no reason why it should not fulfil a similar function in international trade between Member States and countries outside the Community. It will constitute an effective aid to those countries which may not yet be in a position to evaluate independently the merits of a drug they want to import.
It is no exaggeration to conclude that drugs complying with Community standards meet the highest standards which long industrial experience, highly developed scientific and technological skill can put together. Indeed, it is difficult to imagine what further guarantees and documents should be created " to ensure that drugs moving in international commerce meet adequate standards."

NORDIC COUNCIL ON MEDICINES AND COOPERATION ON DRUG CONTROL IN THE NORDIC COUNTRIES

M. Granat

Secretary General Nordic Council on Medicines, Sweden

INTRODUCTION

The purpose of my presentation is to outline the organization of the Nordic Council on Medicines, inform you about some of the results achieved so far, projects running and finally give you an idea of the Nordic cooperation on registration matters.

The Nordic consists of Denmark, Norway, Sweden, Finland and Iceland with a population of 22 million people.

Two elements sustain Nordic cooperation in modern times. Firstly there is a close cultural affinity between our people and our identity of views which is expressed in our systems of law and government. Secondly, our belief in practical and economic advantages of a suitable division of labour and in efficient exploitation of common resources. We work together in practically every sphere of community life. Our joint work takes place at many different levels within associations, firms, organizations, between local authorities and regions and at central government level.

Nordic Council on Medicines

Nordic cooperation in the field of medicines has taken place for many years; especially since the second world war it has developed rapidly. An agreement establishing a free labour market for doctors came into force in 1966 and was followed by similar agreements for dentists, nurses and pharmacists. Agreements were made for elaboration of a Nordic pharmacopoeia. This is today replaced by the European pharmacopoeia. We have common validity of prescriptions. The Nordic Council on Medicines was set up by the Nordic Council of Ministers (ministers of

Social Health and Welfare) in 1975 — that means that the Council has worked so far for seven years.

Mandate

The obligations of the Council are included in the first two articles of the mandate.

Article 1

The Nordic Council on Medicines has been established to harmonize legislation and administrative practices with respect to medicines in the Nordic countries.

Article 2

The main duties of the Council are to:

— propose measures for the harmonization of medical legislation within the Nordic countries

— propose regulations concerning medicines in those instances where administrative authorities are authorized to issue regulations

— propose guidelines for achieving uniform interpretation and implementation of existing medical regulations

— work for the coordination of statistics on medicines

— work for more effective cooperation between the Nordic countries in adverse reaction monitoring

— work for improved cooperation as regards information on medicines

— work for continued cooperation in the field of the pharmacopoeia

— work for the coordination of the Nordic countries contributions within the framework of the European pharmacopoeia

— act as an advisory body to the Health Authorities in the Nordic countries.

The work of the Council does not include the organization of pharmacies, the wholesale trade of drugs or the drug industry.

The organization of the Council

NORDIC COUNCIL ON MEDICINES

— 10 MEMBERS
(2 FROM EACH COUNTRY)

— MEETINGS TWICE A YEAR

— SUB-COMMITTEES

All the member states are represented on the Council with two members from each country. The ten members are appointed by the government of their respective country. The members include medical, pharmaceutical and legal experts. Up to the present, each country has been represented on the Council by at least one member with a leading position in the National Health Service.

SECRETARIAT

— SECRETARY GENERAL

— PROJECT SECRETARY

— 2 ASSISTANTS

The Council is assisted by a secretariat which is directed by a Secretary General and located at the Department of Drugs in Uppsala, Sweden.

The Council meets at least twice a year. According to its statues it draws up the guidelines for its activities and prepares its working programme for each year.

For special duties, the Council sets up sub-committees whose members are appointed by the respective countries, usually not members of the Council. Up to the present, 15 sub-committees have been set up; ten have completed their work. Today five sub-committes are working and the number of people directly involved is about 40 people a year.

The Council is an advisory and coordinating body and, hence, not a supranational organ. Its composition guarantees, however, that decisions reached unanimously by the members can be carried through on a national level relatively quickly. The decisions also show the common opinions of the Nordic countries on different matters.

Nordic drug market

Before presenting some results of our work, let me give you an idea of the drug market.

The number of drugs registered as pharmaceutical specialities in the Nordic countries appears in table 1. The figures refer to different dosage forms and strengths. As you can see it is a fairly low number in comparison with many other countries.

During 1975-1979 there were new drug applications for between 20 to 40 new substances or new combinations of substances each year. Of these about 60 per cent were common for four to five countries. 90% were applied for in two countries. (figure 1). Applications for the registration of new strengths, new dosage forms or changes in previously registered products are not included in the figures. Such applications do not strain the resources of the national regulatory bodies sufficiently to warrant them being the subject of international cooperative projects.

The drug assortments in the Nordic countries are not similar but they are consistent enough to give a good basis for a close cooperation.

Nordic guidelines

We have concentrated our work on the elaboration of common guidelines, such as " Guidelines for clinical trials " and " Guidelines for Registration of Allergen preparations ". In addition we have " Guidelines for the package label ", included nomenclature and definitions for dosage forms.

Table 1. Number of registered Pharmaceutical Specialities, 1980.

	Domestic	Foreign	Totally
Denmark	. .	. .	3 874
Finland	1 845	1 747	3 592
Iceland	6	1 183	1 189
Norway	512	1 444	1 956
Sweden	914	1 545	2 459

There is also a common Nordic decision to give special information on drugs which can affect road-safety as from January 1, 1983. Such drugs will have a triangle on the label together with information and a warning on a package insert.

Nordic Statistics on Medicines

Sales statistics on Medicines have been published in " Nordic Statistics on Medicines " with data for 1975-1977. We are now working on the second edition. This will be available during autumn 1982.

The new edition consists of three parts. Part I contains general information and sales figures for 1978-1980 for about 50 per cent of the drugs registered. Part II is a Nordic drug index.

The drugs are classified according to the Anatomical Therapeutical Chemical classification system (ATC). In part II the " defined daily doses " (DDD) adopted so far will be published together with guidelines for how this statistical unit is worked out. Part III gives the guidelines for the ATC classification.

The methodology of ATC classification and the concept of DDD is now also recommended by the World Health Organization for research on drug utilization.

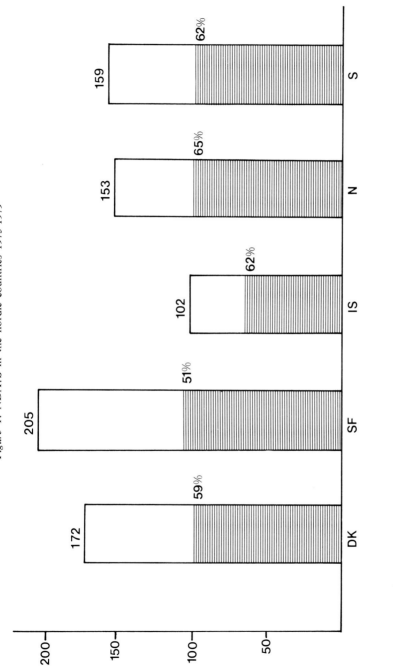

Figure 1. NDA:S in the nordic countries 1975-1979

= COMMON FOR 4 TO 5 COUNTRIES

Projects running

A subcommittee with members from the national drug control authorities is working on guidelines for the preparation of a new drug application. There is also a co-operation on other levels within the field of drug control. The statistics on medicines will be further developed. A closer cooperation on adverse reaction monitoring is under investigation. The traffic warnings on medicines will be coordinated. The pharmacopeia and standardization work will continue. We have also established a notification procedure on new regulations and information activities.

Nordic cooperation on registration

The cooperation within the field of registration of new drugs includes the following items

— Exchange of evaluation reports

— Division of labour on applications

— Continuous information on applications under assessment

— Analysis of decisions

— Yearly meetings between control agencies

— Guidelines for preparation of a new drug application.

The assessments of applications by the regulatory bodies in the Nordic countries are presented in evaluation reports. Those reports give a summarised statement of the submitted documentation together with a conclusion and a recommendation. Such reports are steadily being made more complete and are exchanged between the Nordic control agencies as a routine.

As an example I brought with me an evaluation report on Feldene, Pfizer. It cannot be circulated because it is a confidential paper. It contains about 100 pages and comprises the evaluation of the documentation which was on about 15 000 pages. In this case the assessment was carried out in three countries where each agency was responsible for a certain part of the application.

At the first meeting in Annapolis 1980 Dr Dukes presented these six roads to harmonization

1. Identical drug laws

2. Exchange of internal evaluation reports

3. Division of labour

4. Consultative committee

5. Mutual recognition

6. Supranational agency.

The Nordic approach covers at least the first three of these, maintaining the decision on a national level.

To reach international registration is a difficult task. Instead of starting with a supranational agency the Nordic Countries have chosen a different approach. By harmonizing legislation and guidelines step by step, exchange of evaluation reports and sharing of practical work we aim at a closer cooperation on the control of medicines.

VALUE OF THE MEETING

SUGGESTIONS AND PROPOSALS FOR OTHER ACTIVITIES OF INTERNATIONAL DRUG REGULATORY AUTHORITIES

D. Poggiolini

General Director, Pharmaceutical Division, Ministry of Health, Italy

The Second International Conference of Drug Regulatory Authorities has now reached the end. After four days of intensive work and fruitful exchange of ideas and experiences among all the participants, conclusions have now been approved and a programme for future meetings has also been drafted.

A further step forward was therefore made along the path of cooperation and drug regulation harmonization. Above all, what today may be considered a tradition has been made sound.

Traditions have a remarkable importance both in families and societies; they must not however be considered as a static or decorative element, but as a solid basis for future developments.

I am convinced that the ICDRA tradition will bring us to remarkable and interesting future achievements, and I believe also that with this Second Rome ICDRA a relevant step along this way has been made.

Whatever future developments may be, I am also sure that this cooperation and consultation process among drug regulatory authorities is well started and irreversible.

As Minister Altissimo said at the beginning of our work, only a few years ago all this appeared practically impossible, but thanks to the goodwill of everybody, the cohesion process has become a sound reality.

Drug regulatory authorities have now become fully conscious of the absolute and unquestionable necessity of their close mutual planning inasmuch as their acting in concert may be useful to find the best possible solutions to the problems they have to cope with.

In fact, if political and social problems may be different from one country to another, technical problems linked to health protection are the same all over the world.

It is undoubted and universally recognized that pharmacological progress has brought about enormous benefits to the life of man, achieving also extremely important social improvements. However, as — according to a natural law — no advantage can be obtained without a price to be paid — also in this field, always greater attention is being given to the risks and damages deriving from the use of drugs. Besides, many drugs have progressively proved to be ineffective, outdated, useless, or having remarkable secondary effects.

These secondary effects, sometimes serious, have begun to appear gradually and will be still more frequent in the future having regard to the type of evolution which pharmacotherapy has experienced during recent decades, tending as it does to proliferate molecules which are too close to one another and which are characterized by slight differences, but very often producing secondary effects and toxicological constituents of some importance. This evolution is the consequence of the trend followed in recent years by pharmaceutical research, which concentrated its efforts on the same pharmacological categories, keeping an eye on the foreseeable conditions for pharmacotherapeutical success existing in favourable sectors of the market.

Anyhow, I am convinced that, at the present state of things, more than by any dutiful preliminary test, the safety of a new drug is confirmed and definitely ascertained only by its clinical use.

In this connection, an exchange of information on drugs — and above all on their side effects — to be carried on among regulatory authorities appears to be of paramount importance.

On the basis of these concepts, which everybody is by now grasping, I feel that the moment has come for further developments in this cooperation. How shall we reach them? First of all we have to put a question to ourselves: in which way can drug regulatory authorities give a more useful contribution to this process?

In my opinion, drug regulatory authorities must become fully conscious of their function as drug regulation experts, this activity having endowed them with a baggage of precious and unique experiences gathered during years of work in this sector of public administration.

This rôle therefore makes them responsible not only to the countries they depend on, but also to the citizens of whatsoever country they may belong in order to ensure safe and effective drugs for them.

Undoubtedly, this function has deontological aspects of paramount importance and confers upon the persons who carry it out a particular moral position.

If drug regulatory authorities fully realize all that their rôle implies, they will certainly make every possible effort to always better fulfil it.

What proposals can be made to facilitate this process?

In my opinion, regulatory authorities could contribute to the realization of this purpose, first of all, by more and more fostering their mutual solidarity. This line of conduct involves a question which is above all of a spiritual nature, but which must however be paralleled by practical actions and result in actual achievements.

All this could be accomplished by constituting a drug regulatory authorities'

Association which would help to realize among them that mutual solidarity desired by everybody.

I will try to outline the features this Association might have. It should be a non-profit organization, having only moral aims and a merely un-official character inasmuch as it would not in any way commit or involve governments or international organizations.

The Association should be founded for the sole purpose of the pursuance of community interests.

The objectives of the Association should be the promotion of mutual confidence among drug regulatory authorities with the target to increase knowledge of all kinds, and its rational use in view of anything that is useful to human health.

The sphere of action should be at international level.

The Association should promote studies and research, organize — alone or with the help of other institutions — meetings, seminars, congresses of scientific nature within the province of the regulatory authorities to facilitate their activities and with the aim of finding solutions to their problems.

The organs of the Association could decide on a varied programme and determine to which of the proposed objectives priority must be given.

It is with this in view that the following objectives, in my opinion, should be considered as having priority:

a) the drawing up of reports concerning the evaluation of the use and dangers of pharmaceutical, cosmetic, and chemical preparations as well as foodstuffs, which are internationally on the market, with the purpose of favouring an orderly and balanced development of scientific progress in the general interest of public health;

b) the drawing up of reports concerning the most important economic, political and social problems at international level, particularly in view of the interest of the developing countries;

c) the development, the improvement and the realization of international processes of integration or adaptation and of mutual recognition of regu-lations and decisions governing the pharmaceutical, cosmetic, chemical or food sectors;

d) the development and the realization of new inventions in the above mentioned sectors, which are of pronounced innovative character at inter-national level, by a suitable co-operative programme.

The Association should be autonomous. It should receive no income from economic activities. The Association funds should only be used for the objectives laid down in the Statutes. The members should receive no income from the Association.

Members of the Association could be any physical person, anywhere in the world, encharged with the function of drug regulation. Also persons who were in charge of drug regulation and are now retired or destined to other tasks could belong to the Association. The number of members should be unlimited.

There should be no fees for admission to the Association. The annual membership fee would, however, be a very small amount, for example, ten dollars, to allow the minimum of organizational activity of the Association.

I believe that if you accept these general principles, at least on the whole, and if everybody understands the importance and interest of this initiative, we could go deeper into the question of practical details, such as the drawing up of a real Statute of the Association, which subsequently could be sent to all interested parties in order to obtain useful suggestions and comments.

I am leaving you this thought for reflection and sincerely hope that the discussion which now will follow will bear fruits to help better define the developments of this proposal.

As for myself, all that I wish is that this discussion may conclude in a even more cordial and friendly way a Conference of which — I do hope — you will all keep a good and pleasant recollection.

FINAL REPORT

The Second International Conference was concerned in particular with identifying the legal and scientific framework within which national decisions on drug safety, efficacy, quality, labelling, and information are made, and how these decisions and the basis on which they are formed can be disseminated rapidly to other countries. The Conference sought to identify the measures taken by countries to assure the safety, efficacy and quality of the drugs they export and the requirements for quality control procedures which are applicable to the drugs they import.

The Conference also examined examples of effective regulatory operation in countries with very limited financial and personnel resources. The Conference afforded a valuable opportunity for exchange of information and news on current scientific problems. The Conference considered, inter alia:

(a) what assistance the drug regulatory authorities can provide for each other to facilitate the decision-making process; and

(b) what improvements can be introduced into the drug regulatory facilities in developing countries.

This Report is set out in two parts: the first contains a summary of the discussion that took place during the main proceedings; the second, as an appendix, contains the members' comments along with replies received from 23 countries in response to a questionnaire circulated in advance of the meeting.

A. Assistance in the Decision-Making Process

The fundamental need relates to adequate dissemination of information emanating from developed countries where careful scientific assessments and therapeutic evaluations of new and established drug entities and products have already been performed. The World Health Organization Certification Scheme initiated in 1976 was designed to answer the concerns of importing countries that supplies of drugs would be of good, reliable quality. This was adjudged by the Conference to be most likely if the drug products in question are licensed within the exporting country, especially if the licence has been issued and remains valid on the basis of regular inspections of the manufacturing facilities.

There are a number of appropriate and understandable reasons why a drug may not be licensed for general sale in a given exporting country, for example the regulatory authorities may be awaiting receipt of additional data from the manufacturer to complete the documentation for a licence. Another reason may relate to the absence in the exporting country of the disease entity for which the drug is indicated. As a wide variety of factors underlie decision-making leading to the issue of licences, it is very important for the developing countries importing drugs to make known their specific needs, as well as the progress they have made in the creation and development of drug regulatory procedures.

The WHO Certification Scheme provides a mechanism for documentation of the reasons why a drug is not on sale within the exporting country. It is believed within the Conference that the information already being received on export certificates is highly useful and must be continued. A number of problems, however, have arisen during the implementation period of the Certification Programme. In the case of new pharmaceutical products it is not legally permissible in many jurisdictions to disclose publicly the reasons for refusal of a produce licence, however useful this information would be to importing countries. In most instances information of this type is treated as confidential by regulatory authorities. A simple declaration that a pharmaceutical product is permitted to be sold on the market can be misleading if the declaration hides the fact that it has been allowed to continue to be sold although it has never been evaluated for safety and efficacy according to up-to-date standards. There has been limited participation in the Scheme on the part of regulatory authorities of many importing countries. The reason for this fact is thought to be due to a certain lack of promotion of the Scheme itself, and a second reason may relate to the fact that exporting manufacturers have taken upon themselves the provision of the certification document to facilitate importation into the developing countries. There is a perceived need by some regulatory personnel for additional information on the certification document. Possibly the fact that the primary purpose of the system was assurance of drug quality has, at least to some extent, prevented an extension of the documentation to include factors of safety and efficacy. Last, but not least, there is still a degree of uncertainty within some importing countries about the type of information that they require.

The Conference believes that the Certification Scheme could be rendered even more useful by introducing some minor amendments and additions without engendering the proliferation of documents which are excessively complex.

It is suggested that in addition to the basic information contained on the WHO Certification documents, importing countries should have available supplementary information on any conditions of the licence issued by the exporting country. Enquiries in this area relate to questions with regard to restrictions on use, safety factors including contra-indications, warnings and precautions, and listing of all approved indications. Information of this type is usually available from drug regulatory authorities of the exporting country, from labelling and data sheets, and by means of a perusal of a number of national drug compendia, a detailed listing of which will be available through WHO in the foreseeable future.

In the absence of a data sheet, or a compendium, which states the conditions of registration, a simple request to a drug regulatory authority will result in the immediate availability of all pertinent information. It is usually important for importing countries to receive certification of individual batches of drugs although some countries provide this form of data only for drugs of biological origin. In order to facilitate the ability of drug regulatory authorities to contact each other it is incumbent upon WHO to update and revise the listing of drug regulatory personnel with their titles, addresses, telephone numbers and, where possible, telex codes.

In recent years the Food and Drug Administration of the United States has published a " Summary Basis for Approval " for all new drugs that have been approved for marketing. This invaluable scientific document contains considerable pre-clinical and clinical material which, in most other countries, is regarded as confidential. Many countries are utilizing this document as a part of their decision-making process, although some countries have found that some of the contents are difficult to interpret because of the presence of references to regulations and norms identified by means of numbers and codes.

Still others find the complex scientific data difficult to analyze and use for the evaluation of drug safety and efficacy. Nevertheless, a number of developing countries would greatly appreciate a similar type of document from those exporting countries from which a high proportion of their drugs originates, but whose present drug laws proscribe transmission of data derived from manufacturers applications unless special agreement has been obtained.

In a number of developed countries the format of new drug applications is being changed to include a manufacturer's summary. It is desirable that such a document, possibly amended by national drug regulatory authorities, should in the future be regarded as public in nature and thus transmissible. Whenever a drug has received national clearance or marketing approval within an exporting country, it may be safely assumed that the comprehensive summary document has been adjudged complete and accurate.

There continues to be considerable concern about the standards of manufacturing of drugs destined for export only. Regulations vary from country to country with regard to export licences and the degree to which exported drugs are required to be of identical quality to those marketed within the country of origin. It cannot be too strongly emphasized that quality controls over exported drugs must be maintained by all exporters. It is now recognized that in addition to assurances of manufacturing to pharmacopoeial standards, it is often necessary to have bio-availability tests to demonstrate adequate absorption from the finished product. It has been additionally suggested that a monograph be included on this aspect in all major pharmacopoeias. Documentation of side effects and the listing of indications, warnings and precautions for imported drugs are expected to be essentially identical in content to the information available within the country of origin. It is important that the regulatory authorities of importing countries check the translation of all accompanying directions for use to assure both completeness and consistency.

The World Health Organizations has sought for a number of years to provide a focal point for the exchange of drug information on a global basis between regulatory authorities. Some 15 countries with highly evolved regulatory systems currently contribute to this scheme. These data are utilized for dissemination to all Member States, sometimes in the form of special newsletters and in a more expanded form in Drug Information Bulletins. The data relate both to acceptance criteria for new drugs and to restrictions and withdrawals. These forms of communication continue to be widely appreciated and utilized by health professionals and regulatory agencies worldwide.

While all existing pathways should continue, it is believed that it is now timely to recommend a more extensive and selective list of informational components. Indeed, such a list was submitted to the Conference by the representative from Indonesia.

B. Improvement of Drug Regulatory Facilities in Developing Countries

A number of WHO and UNIDO fellowships continue to be awarded, and consultations are arranged on an ad hoc basis. Obviously these should be continued, although there is now need for an expansion of the areas of expertise possessed by these persons. For example, management training is now considered essential. The existence of a well prepared core staff that can guarantee efficient administration and operation of the Agency, in addition to scientific expertise, is an obvious key point for the functioning of any drug regulatory agency. Recently WHO has emphasized the need for competent management of complex data.

International non-proprietary names for drugs should be used by all agencies and should be made compulsory as supplementary brand names for industry. Nomenclature problems are, in some deleloping countries, a continuing major source of confusion.

It is emphasized that the training of personnel in highly sophisticated biochemical techniques may not help to achieve the practical competence that is required in the much less well equipped laboratories of most developing countries. It is thus important that the curriculum of study for all trainees be carefully planned and defined, possibly on the basis of a preliminary fact-finding visit to the developing country to assess actual needs and conditions of work prior to commencement of training.

The establishment of regional laboratories appears to be a most useful adjunct for developing countries. A model already exists in Jamaica for use by all Caribbean countries, and in Africa a network of laboratories concerned with vaccines is in the process of establishment. Details of analytical methodology used for a specific drug are best obtained from the regulatory authority within the exporting country.

Continuing government-sponsored programmes and a recent generous offer by some sections of the international pharmaceutical industry to help train personnel, should lead to an improvement of expertise available in drug regulatory laboratories. The arrangements that have been made by some developed countries to send qualified staff to some developing countries to train local personnel in drug regulatory affairs is to be highly commended, as is a trend towards the hosting of regulatory personnel from developing countries within laboratories of developed countries.

All training of this type, whether undertaken within developed countries, or locally in developing countries, is likely to be more satisfactory if it is based upon an agreed curriculum. The Conference recommends that WHO undertake the preparation of a special publication such as a " Curriculum for Essential Laboratory Training ".

In addition to specific periods of technical and management training, which may last several years, a number of shorter courses and regional seminars are recommended to assure updating of personnel in rapidly advancing methodologies. The Conference contends that the establishment by developing countries of their own pharmaceutical manufacturing facilities would contribute greatly to the solution of many local problems concerning the quality assurance of drugs.

C. Future Operational Planning and Coordination

It is considered essential that the standing committee recommended in the report of the ICDRA meeting in Annapolis, Maryland, be established promptly. It is the intention that this standing committee would participate with the host country in the planning of the programme for future ICDRA meetings, in the preparation of necessary background papers, and that it should be charged with the taking of such steps as may be open to it to secure the implementation of Conference recommendations. In addition, the standing committee would advise WHO on matters concerning drug information and regulation as originally recommended by the Geneva meeting of December 4-6, 1979.

REVIEW OF REPLIES TO QUESTIONNAIRES, AND ANALYSIS OF SIMILAR APPROACHES TO DRUG REGISTRATION AND SIGNIFICANT DIFFERENCES

The Conference reviewed the replies received from 25 countries to a questionnaire on the structure and functions of their drug regulatory agencies. It noted that although the definition of the substances subject to regulatory control varied from country to country, they were all consonant with the definition contained in the WHO TRS No: 567, 1975 (*). Drug regulatory authorities represented at the Conference were mainly concerned with the control of drugs which are related to the protection of human health; these include drugs either of natural or chemical origin, biologicals, narcotics and drugs for veterinary use that could have an impact of human health. The common objective of the national control authorities being to ensure the quality, safety and efficacy of drugs available within the country, the Conference noted that the extent to which the authorities also controlled drugs for export, particularly with regard to quality and labelling, varied from country to country. For importing countries with limited resources, it was very important to know whether the regulatory authorities exerted controls on all exported drugs or only on some of them (e.g. psychotropic drugs in accordance with the 1971 Convention) and whether such controls were, or were not, of the same character as for drugs on the domestic market.

The Conference noted that in about one-half of the countries responding, the regulatory authorities also considered the price of the drugs in reviewing the application for the marketing authorization, while in other countries the price was not considered at the time of drug registration.

(*) Any substance or mixture of substances that is manufactured, sold, offered for sale, or represented for use in: (1) the treatment, mitigation, prevention, or diagnosis of disease, an abnormal physical state or the symptoms thereof in man or animal; or (2) the restoration, correction, or modification of organic functions in man or animal.

The control of quality, safety and efficacy was implemented in most countries in accordance with the same basic principles, but the legislative basis for such controls, the structure of the regulatory agency and the functions of the agency varied from country to country depending on political, economic and social conditions and was a matter for national decision. As far as the financial aspects were concerned, the Conference was of the opinion that the figures provided by the countries for the domestic market and the values of drugs exported or imported gave an order of magnitude even if they were not precise. It should be realized, however, that a drug market size did not necessarily relate to the health needs of the population; the correlation was not obtainable from the questionnaires. The harmonization of scientific and technical aspects of drug regulation is a first priority and the exchange of information on scientific issues is a step in this direction.

Some problems with regard to quality assurance were discussed and it was emphasized that substantial progress has been made over the past ten years in GMP and analytical controls, and therefore importing countries should pay attention to the date of registration or revision when they select products.

The Conference considered that national drug regulatory control agencies were increasingly confronted in many countries with the question of regulating traditional remedies, either locally produced or imported. Although these products may have been used for a long time, it was important to ensure that they were safe. As far as efficacy was concerned, most countries did not apply the same requirements as for a new drug. The requirements for control of the safety and quality of traditional remedies, where they exist, vary widely among countries. Ideally, scientific methods should be used in the evaluation of these remedies, but the nature of the substances and the patterns of use render this difficult. For imported traditional remedies there is an increasing need for the exchange of information.

QUESTIONNAIRE TABLE

SECOND INTERNATIONAL CONFERENCE OF DRUG REGULATORY AUTHORITIES QUESTIONNAIRE TABLE

Country	Legis. Basis yes	no	Total	Doc.	Ph.	Sc.	Law	Ad.	Cl.	N. Auth. (D)	Ins. (D)	Rew. (C)	Adv. Com. yes	no	Export yes	no	Import yes	no	Need Clause yes	no	Price yes	no	Restrict. lists yes	no	Hospit. Formul. yes	no
Australia	★		74	16	10	14		2	32	120	100	no	★		★			★		★		★		★	★	
Austria	★		(I)	(I)	(I)	(I)	(I)	(I)	(I)	232	30	yes	★		★		★		★		★		★		★	
Barbados	★		(I)	(I)	(I)	(I)	(I)	(I)	(I)	(I)	(I)	(I)	(I)		★		★		(I)		(I)		(I)		★	
Brazil	★		69	13	12	1		1	42	2136	(Q)	yes	★		★		★		(I)		(I)		(I)		(I)	
Canada	★		436	25	46	145		17	201	95	302	yes	★			★	★			★		★		★	★	
Chile	★		63	29			2		34	512	(F)	yes	★		★		★		★		★		★			★
Federal Rep. of Germany	★		264	33	36	17	2	51	125	1050	Fed. States		★		★ Fed. St.		★ Fed. St.			★		★	★		★	
Finland	★		31	4	18	2	(I)	(I)	6	3600	(E)	yes	★		★		★			★		★		★	★	
France	★		145	(I)	(I)	(I)	(I)	(I)	(I)	277	(I)	yes	★		★		★			★		★		★	★	
Greece	★		58	2/3	34	21	(I)	(I)	(I)	385	(E)	yes	★			★	★		★			★	★			★
Hungary	★		148	79				21	48	1300 (L, H)	(M)	yes	★			★	★		★			★		★		★
Iceland	★		6	4					2	100	3	yes	★		★		★			★		★		★	★	

Country																				
Indonesia	★	269	58	8	3	10	190	750	50	yes	★	★	★	★	★	★	★	★	★	★
Israel	★	60 (B)	12	20	25	(B)	15	400	100	yes	★	★	★	★	★	★	★	★	★	★
Italy	★	127	3	17	14	12	72	150	87	yes	★	★	★	★	★	★	★	★	★	★
Japan	★	165	56				106	4123	3696	yes	★	★	★	★	★	★	★	★	★	★
Libya	★	(I)	(I)	(I)	(I)	(I)	(I)	(I)	(I)	yes	★	★	★	★	★	★			★	★
Netherlands	★	48	8	6	8	1	25	190	50	yes	★	★	★	★	★	★	★	★	★	★
New Zealand	★	19	3	1	11		4	168	48	no	★	(A)	★	★	★	★	★		★	
Norway	★	48	19	6		20	200	5-6		yes	★	★	★	★	★	★	★	★	★	★
South Africa	★	31	2	14		15	235	167		yes	★	★	★	★	★	★	★	★	★	★
Sweden	★	165	21	21	28		74	105	41	yes	★	★	★	★	★	★	★	★	★	★
U. K.	★	315	21	50	37	4	60	894 (G)	1000	yes	★	★	★	★	★	★	★	★	★	★
U.S.A.	★	1077 (N)	98	44	462	151	309	363	4900 (F)	yes	★	★	★	★	★	★	★	★ (O)	★ (P)	★
Zimbabwe	★	11	5	4	2		1538 (H)	(I)	(I)	no	★	(A)	★	★	★	★	★	★	★	★

(A) except for narcotics
(B) yes, part-time
(C) number not reported
(D) average recent years
(E) once a year for each laboratory
(F) once every two years for each laboratory
(G) 129 for animals
(H) total number of drugs registered

(I) no information
(L) 30 per year
(M) twice per year for each laboratory
(N) for headquarters
(O) yes, for some States
(P) some hospitals do and some do not
(Q) never been done

LIST OF PARTICIPANTS *

* This list is intended to facilitate communication between Regulatory Authorities.

Name of Participant	Country	Title	Full Address	N. Phone	N. Telex
A. S. Abdulwahid	Saudi Arabia	Ministry of Health-Medical Licenses and Pharmaceutical Affairs	Ministry of Health, Medical Licences and Pharmaceutical Affairs - Riyadh	Home: 4037829	00459/201628
K. Adank	Switzerland	Head Registration and Evaluation service	Intercantonal Office for the Control of Medicaments Erlachstr. 8 CH - 3000 Berne 9	031/230105	—
A. A. K. Al-Asbahi	Yemen Arab Republic	Director Registration Division	Ministry of Health Yemen P.O. Box n. 1150 - Sana	76461 - 76460	2381
S. L. Alba	Panama	Ie/e de la Sección de la Farmacias y Drogas	Farmacias y Drogas - Ministerio de la Salud APDO 2048	25-3327	3127 - Ofsanpan PG
F. S. Antezana Aranibar	Who - Geneva	Senior Scientist - DAP-DTR	Avenue Appia, Geneva 27	913649-913648	27821 V OMS CH
A. Y. Baqer	Kuwait	Pharmacist	Center of Quality, Control and Registration Ministry of Public Health	545141, 832087	33291
I. Bayer	Hungary	Director General National Institute of Pharmacy	1372 Budapest 5 - Zrinyi n. 3; P.O. Box 450	171-462	224656 - OGYI-H
N. Bel	E.E.C.	Head of Division Commission European Communities	Rond Point Schuman 3 - Brussels 1040	02/2351891	25768

Name of Participant	Country	Title	Full Address	N. Phone	N. Telex
F. S. Boi-Doku	Congo	Regional Officer, HLS, WHO Africa	WHO Regional Officer for Africa, P.B.L. - Brazzaville		
G. R. Boyd	New Zealand	Deputy Director Division of Clinical Services	Department of Health P.O. Box 5013 - Wellington	727-627	NZ - 3571
A. Breit	Austria	Director	Federal Ministry of Health and Enviromental Protection - 1030 Vienna	222-725641 ext.	131300
C. H. Calvete	Argentina	Asessor de Gabinete de Subsecretaria de Medicina Social y Fiscalizazion Sanitaria	Defensa 120 O.F. 4074 1345 Buenos Aires	303304	—
R. Capasso	Italy	Dirigente Superiore Chimico	Direzione Generale Servizio Farmaceutico Ministero della Sanità Viale Civiltà Romana, 7 00144 Roma - E.U.R.	06-5925828	Minsan I 610453
Chang Yu-Pei	People's Rep. of China	First Secretary in the Embassy of People's Rep. of China in Italy	Via A. Morelli, 5 - Roma	(06) 80.20.59	—
E. Chidomere	Nigeria	Chief Drug Inspecting Officer	Food and Drugs Administration, Federal Ministry of Health P.M.B. 2022 - Yaba-Lagos	91-684071	—
T. Chrusciel	Poland	Professor of Pharmacology, MD, Deputy Director of the Institute	Drug Research and Control Institute Chelmska 30/34 - Warszawa	415303	—

Name of Participant	Country	Title	Full Address	N. Phone	N. Telex
D. Cook	Canada	Director General Drugs Directorate	Health Protection Branch Tunne's Pasture KIA OL2	613/731-6795	053-3679 HWC HPB OTT
J. Dangoumau	France	Directeur de la Pharmacie et des Medicaments	Ministère de la Santé I Place Fontenoy - 75007 Paris	(1) 567.55.44	Santsec 25001 IF
M. Daskalakis	Greece	President of Keep (National Laboratory of Drugs)	Keep Voulis 4 - Athens	3235377	215927 YKYP GR
E. Diaz Espina	Venezuela	Jefe del Departamento de Registro de Productos Farmaceuticos	Division Drogas y Cosmeticos, Ministerio de Sanidad, Edificio Sur Centro Simon Bolivar Caracas	4834377-919185	—
M. N. G. Dukes	WHO (European Region)	Regional Officer for Pharmaceuticals	Scherfigsvej 8, 2100, Kobenhavn, Denmark	(01) 290111	32691
J. F. Dunne	WHO Headquarters	Chief, Pharmaceuticals Division Diagnostic, Therapeutic and Rehabilitative Technology	WHO, Avenue Appia, 1211 Geneva 27	913662	27821 V OMS CH
M. Effentakis	Greece	Pharmacist	Ministry of Social Services Aristotelous 17 - Athens	5237483	21597 YKYP GR
V. Fattorusso	Italy		1111 - Tolochenaz - Suisse	(021) 71.37.24	—

Name of Participant	Country	Title	Full Address	N. Phone	N. Telex
K. Feiden	Fed. Rep. of Germany	Ministerialrat	Federal Ministry of Youth, Family & Health Deutschherrenstr, 87 D- 5300 Bonn	228-3381	885437 bmjfg d
F. Ferrandiz	Spain	Pharmacist Ph. D.	Comision Asesora Cientifica y Tecnica c/ Fermin Caballero 62 - 4° c, Madrid 3Y	4112112 - 2018986	—
P. Fischer	Switzerland	Dr. iur. Director	Intercantonal Office for the Control of Medicaments (INS) Erlachstr, 8 CH - 3000 Berne 9	031-230105	—
P. I. Folb	South Africa	Prof. (Chairperson, South African Medicines Control Council)	Department of Clinical Pharmacology, University of Cape Town Medical School, Observatory 7925	021-472350 ext. 25 (Home 921-693336)	SA 3676
D. Galletis	Zimbabwe	Registrar of Drugs	Drugs Control Council P.O. Box UA 559 Union Avenue - Salisbury	708255 - 792165	—
M. Garcia-Sainz	Mexico	Director General de Control de Alimentos, Bebides y Medicamentos	Liverpool 80, Colonia Juarez Mexico 4 D.F.	525 1253 525 1574	—
N. M. Ghannan	Saud Arabia	Pharmacist Registration Division	Pharmaceutical Affairs, Ministry of Helath - Riyadh	47754 - 4069185	—

Name of Participant	Country	Title	Full Address	N. Phone	N. Telex
R. Gonzales	Chile	Jefe Dpto. Control Nacional Instituto Salud Publica	Maraton 1000 - Santiago	2236281	—
R. Gonzales Oti	Spain	Director General de la Farmacia y Medicamentos	Ministerio de Sanidad y Consumo Paseo del Prado 18-20 Madrid 14	227.6700 2281899	44014
M. Granat	Sweden	Secretary General	Nordic Council on Medicines Box 607, S-75252 Uppsala	18 - 100360	—
J. P. Griffin	United Kingdom	Senior Principal Medical Officer (Professional Head of Medicines Division)	(Rm, 1628) Market Towers Department of Health 1, Nine Elms Lane London SW8 SNQ	01-720-2188 ext. 3133, 3134	883669
S. T. Gudmundsson	Iceland	M. D., Chairman Icelandic Committee on Pharmaceuticals	Dept. of Medicines, Landspitalinn University Hosp. Reykiavik	(Area code Iceland) 29000, X 384	2090 VESSEL IS
J. A. Halperin	U.S.A.	Deputy Director Bureau of Drugs Food, Drug Administration	5600 Fishers Lane, Rockville, Maryland 28832	301-443-2894 Home: 301-774-2416	898-488 PHS/ PKLN/ROV
F. Magne Halse	Norway	Director	National Center for Medicinal Products Control Sven Oftedals Vei 6, Oslo 9	(02) 257550	—

Name of Participant	Country	Title	Full Address	N. Phone	N. Telex
I. Henderson	Canada	Director Bureau Human Prescription	Tower B - Place Vanier 355 River Rd., Vanier Ontario KIA - 1B8	613-992-4684; Home 613-256-1631	Same as Health Protect. Branch Central Number 053-3679 HWC HPB OTT
B. Huyghe	Belgium	Inspecteur Générale de la Pharmacie	Ministère de la Santé Quarter Vésale, 1010 Brussels	02-5641064	25768
G. Kristinsdottir	Iceland	Secretary of the Committee on Pharmaceuticals - Pharmacist	Committee on Pharmaceuticals, Is, Lugavegur 116 - 105 Reykjavik	(91) 28455	—
L. Ibarra	Venezuela	Farmacologo Clinico, Jefe Seccion Farmacologia Clinica	Instituto Nacional de Higiene Ciudad Universitaria Caracas, Apartado 60, 412 - Oficina del Este	620921 - 619811 ext. 2285 Hab. 214204	—
J. Idanpaan-Heikkila	Finland	Chief Medical Officer for Pharmacology	National Board of Health (Health Directorate of Finland) Siltasaarenkatu 18 00530 Helsinki 53	90-718511	121774 NBH SF
O. Issa	Libya	Head of Pharmaceutical and Drug Research Section	Pharmacy & Medical Equipment Dept. Secretariat of Health, Tripoli	605151-56	20381 Health Ly
B. Jøldal	Norway	Director Pharmaceutical Division	The Health Services of Norway P.O. Box 8128, N- Oslo Dep.	2-119090	—

Name of Participant	Country	Title	Full Address	N. Phone	N. Telex
M. Legrain	France	President de la Commission d'Autorisation des Medicaments	Hopital la Pitiè 83, Bvd., de l'Hopital 75634 Paris - Cedex 13	584 14 12 5401	—
V. Longo	Italy	Direttore Laboratorio di Farmacologia Ist. Superiore Sanità - Roma			
J. Loutsch-Weydert	Luxembourg	Chef de la Division de la Pharmacie et du Medicaments	Direction de la Santé 28, Bvd. Joseph II 1840 Luxembourg	47.55.01	25 46 SANTE LU
G. N. Mahlangu	Zimbabwe		Drugs Control Council P.O. Box UA 559 Union Avenue - Harare	708255 26731 ext 204	—
L. Mintoff	Malta	Senior Pharmacist & Secretary Drugs and Therapeutics Committee	Ministry of Health - Valletta	24701	—
H. Nakajima	Philippines	WHO Regional Director WHO Regional Office for Western Pacific	P.O. Box 2932		27652 WHO PH
S. C. Opara	Nigeria	Assistant Director Drug Control	Food and Drugs Administration Federal Ministry of Health - Koyi	91-684071	—
J. Øverø	Denmark	Deputy Director-General Chief Pharmacist	Sundhedsstyrelsen 1, St. Kongensgade 1264 Copenhagen	01-141011	31316 SERUM DK

Name of Participant	Country	Title	Full Address	N. Phone	N. Telex
D. Poggiolini	Italy	General Director Pharmaceutical Division	Ministry of Health Viale della Città Romana, 7 00144 Roma E.U.R.	(06) 5925863 5925824	Minsan I 610453
F. Pocchiari	Italy	Direttore Istituto Superiore Sanità - Roma			
L. Robert	EEC	Chairman of the EEC Committee for Proprietary Medicinal Products	18 Rue J. P. Koening Luxembourg	260.76	—
F. A. El Said Saleh	Egypt	Pharmaceutical Inspector Division	Ministry of Public Health Pharmaceutical Sector - Cairo	29.802	—
B. Sankaran	WHO Headquarters	Director Division Diagnostic Therapeutic and Rehabilitative Technology	Avenue Appia 1211 Geneva 27		27821 V OMS CH
B. Schnieders	Fed. Rep. of Germany	Professor und Leiter des Instituts fuer Arzneimittel des BGA	Seestraße 10 1000 Berlin 65	(030) 4502-203	183310
P. S. Schönhöfer	Fed. Rep. of Germany	Prof. Dr.	Bundesgesundheitsamt, Inst. f. Arzneimittel Stauffenbergstr. 13 D-1000 Berlin 30	(30) 263 7249	183310
H. Seiler	Switzerland	Dr. Med. Adjoint Scientifique	Federal Office for Public Health Bollwerk, 27 - 3001 Berne	(031) 619649	33880 ofspch

Name of Participant	Country	Title	Full Address	N. Phone	N. Telex
K. Shirota	Japan	Director Evaluation and Registration Division Pharmaceutical Affairs Bureau	Ministry 67 Health and Welfare 1-2-2, Kasumigaseki Chiyodaku - Tokyo	03-503-1711	222-5132
M. P. Sihombing	Indonesia	Director Drug Control FDA	Ministry of Health Jl. Percetakan Negara 23 - Jakarta	414947	44382 KAFARMA IAT
S. Soesilo	Indonesia	Subdirector for Drug Registration	Directorate General for Drug & Food Control Jl. Percetakan Nagara, 23 - Jakarta pusat	(021) 415459	44382 KAFARMA IAT
K. Strandberg	Sweden	Director Division of Pharmacotherapeutics	National Board of Health & Welfare Dept. of Drugs Box 607 - S-75125 - Uppsala	018-100360	—
M. Ten Ham	Netherlands	Deputy Secretary	Dutch Board for the Evaluation of Medicines P.O. Box 5811 2290 HV Rijswijk (2H)	070-949505	32691
N. Van Der Merwe	South Africa	Registrar of Medicines Medicines Control Council	Private Bag X63 - Pretoria	282851	0095/3676/SA
A. Vila-Coro Barrachina	Spain	Subdirector General Establecimientos y Asistencia Pharmaceutica	Ministerio de Sanidad y Consumo - 9a Planta Paseo del Prado 18 - Madrid 14	467 - 34 - 28	44014

Name of Participant	Country	Title	Full Address	N. Phone	N. Telex
E. Weisenberg	Israel	Director, Institute of Control and Standardization of Drugs	P.O.B. 1457 - Jerusalem	(02) 24.74.02	26137 HEAL IL
R. N. Williams	United Kingdom	Administrative Head of Medicines Division Dept. of Health & Social Security Medicines Division	Market Towers 1 Nine Elms Lane London SW8 5NQ	01-720-2188	883669
R. E. Wilson	Australia	Assistant Director - General Therapeutic Goods Branch	Commonwealth Department of Health - P.O. Box 100 - Woden, A.C.T. 2606	(062) 899538	AA 62149
A.C. Zanini	Brazil	National Secretary	Vigilancia Sanitaria Ministério de Saúde 70058 Esplanada Ministerios Brasilia	(061) 226.9961	611251